CW00742796

The Political Economy of the Egyptian Revolution

DOI: 10.1057/9781137395924

Other Palgrave Pivot titles

Michael J. Osborne: Multiple Interest Rate Analysis: Theory and Applications

Barry Stocker: Kierkegaard on Politics

Lauri Rapeli: The Conception of Citizen Knowledge in Democratic Theory

Michele Acuto and Simon Curtis: Reassembling International Theory: Assemblage Thinking and International Relations

Stephan Klingebiel: Development Cooperation: Challenges of the New Aid Architecture

Mia Moody-Ramirez and Jannette Dates: The Obamas and Mass Media: Race, Gender, Religion, and Politics

Kenneth Weisbrode: Old Diplomacy Revisited

Christopher Mitchell: Decentralization and Party Politics in the Dominican Republic

Keely Byars-Nichols: The Black Indian in American Literature

Vincent P. Barabba: Business Strategies for a Messy World: Tools for Systemic Problem-Solving

Cristina Archetti: Politicians, Personal Image and the Construction of Political Identity: A Comparative Study of the UK and Italy

Mitchell Congram, Peter Bell and Mark Lauchs: Policing Transnational Organised Crime and Corruption: Exploring Communication Interception Technology

János Kelemen: The Rationalism of Georg Lukács

Patrick Manning: Big Data in History

Susan D. Rose: Challenging Global Gender Violence: The Global Clothesline Project

Thomas Janoski: Dominant Divisions of Labor: Models of Production That Have Transformed the World of Work

Gray Read: Modern Architecture in Theater: The Experiments of Art et Action

Robert Frodeman: Sustainable Knowledge: A Theory of Interdisciplinarity

Antonio V. Menéndez Alarcón: French and US Approaches to Foreign Policy

Stephen Turner: American Sociology: From Pre-Disciplinary to Post-Normal

Ekaterina Dorodnykh: Stock Market Integration: An International Perspective

Bill Lucarelli: Endgame for the Euro: A Critical History

Mercedes Bunz: The Silent Revolution: How Digitalization Transforms Knowledge, Work, Journalism and Politics without Making Too Much Noise

Kishan S. Rana: The Contemporary Embassy: Paths to Diplomatic Excellence

Mark Bracher: Educating for Cosmopolitanism: Lessons from Cognitive Science and Literature

Carroll P. Kakel III: The Holocaust as Colonial Genocide: Hitler's 'Indian Wars' in the 'Wild East'

Laura Linker: Lucretian Thought in Late Stuart England: Debates about the Nature of the Soul

Nicholas Birns: Barbarian Memory: The Legacy of Early Medieval History in Early Modern Literature

Adam Graycar and Tim Prenzler: Understanding and Preventing Corruption

Michael J. Pisani: Consumption, Informal Markets, and the Underground Economy: Hispanic Consumption in South Texas

DOI: 10.1057/9781137395924

palgrave▸pivot

The Political Economy of the Egyptian Revolution: Mubarak, Economic Reforms and Failed Hegemony

Roberto Roccu
Lecturer, King's College London, UK

palgrave
macmillan

DOI: 10.1057/9781137395924

© Roberto Roccu 2013

All rights reserved. No reproduction, copy or transmission of this publication may be made without written permission.

No portion of this publication may be reproduced, copied or transmitted save with written permission or in accordance with the provisions of the Copyright, Designs and Patents Act 1988, or under the terms of any licence permitting limited copying issued by the Copyright Licensing Agency, Saffron House, 6–10 Kirby Street, London EC1N 8TS.

Any person who does any unauthorized act in relation to this publication may be liable to criminal prosecution and civil claims for damages.

The author has asserted his right to be identified as the author of this work in accordance with the Copyright, Designs and Patents Act 1988.

First published 2013 by
PALGRAVE MACMILLAN

Palgrave Macmillan in the UK is an imprint of Macmillan Publishers Limited, registered in England, company number 785998, of Houndmills, Basingstoke, Hampshire RG21 6XS.

Palgrave Macmillan in the US is a division of St Martin's Press LLC, 175 Fifth Avenue, New York, NY 10010.

Palgrave Macmillan is the global academic imprint of the above companies and has companies and representatives throughout the world.

Palgrave® and Macmillan® are registered trademarks in the United States, the United Kingdom, Europe and other countries

ISBN: 978-1-137-39593-1   EPUB
ISBN: 978-1-137-39592-4   PDF
ISBN: 978-1-137-39591-7   Hardback

This book is printed on paper suitable for recycling and made from fully managed and sustained forest sources. Logging, pulping and manufacturing processes are expected to conform to the environmental regulations of the country of origin.

A catalogue record for this book is available from the British Library.

A catalog record for this book is available from the Library of Congress.

DOI: 10.1057/9781137395924

Contents

DOI: 10.1057/9781137395924

Acknowledgements

This little volume is the result of four years of research conducted at both the London School of Economics and Political Science (LSE) and King's College London. Within the former, I am particularly grateful to Kimberly Hutchings and Federica Bicchi for their acute comments, which undoubtedly improved this work, and the unfailing moral support at various stages during the process. Since I have become part of it in September 2012, the Department of European and International Studies at King's College has provided an immensely stimulating environment where the book has taken shape in its final form. I am particularly thankful to both my formal mentor Simona Talani and my 'summer mentor' Magnus Ryner for the many discussions which, directly or otherwise, have fed back into this work. And I look forward to many more. Comments from Charles Tripp, Toby Dodge and George Lawson also contributed significantly in making this work a better one.

I am very thankful also to all my colleagues and friends in both institutions for taking the time to discuss some of the ideas contained in the book and most importantly for always being there in the unavoidable moments of despair. Some of them deserved to be singled out for both their sharpness and patience. These are Damiano De Felice, Philippe Fournier, Joe Hoover, Bona Muzaka, Gonzalo Pozo, Meera Sabaratnam, Laust Schouenborg and Benedetta Voltolini.

My several stays in Cairo have been made much more enjoyable and productive by discussions with many friends. Among these, a particular mention is due to Farid Abdeen, Holger Albrecht, Marco Masulli, Marco Pinfari and the late Samer Soliman, whose relentless political activism is missed as much as the depth and subtlety of his academic work.

Christina Brian and Amanda McGrath at Palgrave Macmillan have been superb in combining understanding for my recurring delays with gentle pressure applied with a smile when the typescript was needed. I doubt I could have ever hoped for a better editorial team to work with.

Doctoral research in London would not have been possible without the scholarships from the Sardinian Regional Government (*Regione Autonoma Sardegna*) and the Department of International Relations at LSE. My family provided me with vital funds during my first months in London, and most crucially with unreserved support, affection and much needed humour throughout the years. This work is dedicated to them, and to Mihaela and Daniela, whose love and companionship in different phases of this long project has been much more important to me than I could ever hope to put down in words.

DOI: 10.1057/9781137395924

List of Abbreviations

AmCham	American Chamber of Commerce in Egypt
ARE	Arab Republic of Egypt
BRIC	Brazil, Russia, India, China
CBE	Central Bank of Egypt
EBA	Egyptian Businessmen's Association
ECES	Egyptian Center for Economic Studies
EGX	Egyptian Exchange
EIU	Economist Intelligence Unit
ERF	Economic Research Forum
ERSAP	Economic Reform and Structural Adjustment Programme
FEMISE	Euromediterranean Forum of Economics Institutes (*Forum Euroméditerranéen des Instituts des Sciences Économiques*)
FJP	Freedom and Justice Party
HIECS	Household Income, Expenditure and Consumption Survey
IFI	international financial institution
IPE	International Political Economy
IR	International Relations
LCHR	Land Center for Human Rights
LE	Egyptian pound
MALR	Ministry of Agriculture and Land Reclamation
MEED	Middle East Economic Digest
NDP	National Democratic Party
NPL	non-performing loan
NSDP	National Supplier Development Programme

DOI: 10.1057/9781137395924

PBDAC   Principal Bank for Development and Agricultural Credit
PPP   public-private partnership
SCAF   Supreme Council of the Armed Forces
SOE   state-owned enterprise
UNDP   United Nations Development Programme
USAID   US Agency for International Development
WDI   World Development Indicators

DOI: 10.1057/9781137395924

Introduction: Bread, Dignity, Social Justice and Economic Reforms

Abstract: *After surveying the literature on the causes of the Egyptian revolution, the introduction outlines the main argument of this book, suggesting that economic reforms implemented since the late 1980s created an ever greater polarisation within the regime and in society at large. In so doing, these reforms created some of the socio-economic preconditions for the popular uprisings leading to the fall of Mubarak.*

Keywords: Egyptian revolution; economic reforms; causality; methods

Roccu, Roberto. *The Political Economy of the Egyptian Revolution: Mubarak, Economic Reforms and Failed Hegemony.* Basingstoke: Palgrave Macmillan, 2014. DOI: 10.1057/9781137395924.

'This time is different'. On a torrid Sunday in early July 2010, sitting on a large armchair in his opulent and indulgently air-conditioned office in Heliopolis, then minister of investment Mahmoud Mohieldin gave what felt like a routine answer to what probably was a routine question. Echoing the concerns of the respected economist Hanaa Kheir-el-Din, I asked the minister whether also in this occasion the push for reform was receding with the first improvements, as some measures taken in 2009 and 2010 already seemed to suggest. 'This time is different' was his answer, before he eloquently went on to claim that the halt in reforms was due to adverse global economic conditions, and that the impetus for reforms would have gathered new momentum as soon as the global economy would allow for it. After all, he suggested that the cabinet was still the same, and so were the beliefs of its most prominent members.[1]

A couple of months after our interview, the president of the World Bank Robert Zoellick appointed Mohieldin as managing director of the World Bank group, praising him as 'a tireless reformer' and '[a]n outstanding young leader' (World Bank 2010c). Mohieldin took his post in early October, thus resigning (first minister in the history of republican Egypt) from the Ministry of Investment whose policy remit had been tailored around his competences and projects. About three-and-a-half months later, while Mohieldin was in his new office in Washington, DC, hundreds of thousands people demonstrated around the streets of Cairo, Alexandria and other major cities in Egypt asking for an end to 30 years of emergency law. As days went on, the protests increased both in size and demands, leading, on 11 February 2011, to the resignation of Hosni Mubarak after almost three decades of rule.

Mohieldin had been proven right in two ways. The obvious meaning of his statement, as witnessed by his following remarks, was that a 'reformist' cabinet had finally emerged in Egypt and proved able to discard a state-dominated economy.[2] The support given by the army to demonstrators in the first phase of the revolution could then be seen as the reaction on the part of the *ancien régime* against the 'winner-take-all' tendencies of the new bourgeoisie empowered by reforms. Mohieldin was also right in a way he had not intended. This time was different because the impact of both the wide-ranging reforms implemented over the past two decades and the global economic crisis, though not captured adequately by the aggregate indicators provided in official reports, had led a substantial portion of the Egyptian middle and lower classes to desperation and eventually to take to the streets. Reforms driven by neoliberal ideas, and

DOI: 10.1057/9781137395924

the effects of the crisis of the neoliberal economic model worldwide, had succeeded in mobilising Egyptian masses against their rulers.

Following Mohieldin's suggestion, this work looks at the economic reforms carried out in Egypt in the 1990s and 2000s in order to understand what was different this time, and why.

The causes of the Egyptian revolution: surveying the literature

Very few political commentators and academics have demonstrated prescience in anticipating the Arab uprisings of late 2010 and early 2011. In the case of Egypt, John Bradley certainly stands out for seeing how conditions had changed in most aspects of Egyptian social life, effectively bringing the country 'on the brink of a revolution' (2008). Whereas he is arguably the only author who clearly saw it coming, there have been other works, such as for example the edited collection by El-Mahdi and Marfleet (2009), which had highlighted the emergence of a set of conditions that were considered likely to put under increasing pressure the existing authoritarian arrangement. This awareness was however tempered by the enduring repressive power of the state and the heritage of decades of systematic political demobilisation.

As it often happens, predictive failure has swiftly been compensated by the emergence of a rather sizeable *ex post* literature addressing the causes of the Arab uprisings in general and of the Egyptian revolution more specifically. The reasons for the abundance of these accounts are to a great degree understandable. In less than a month, two of the longest-ruling autocrats in the Middle East had been toppled by popular upheavals, with consequences in the region ranging from unsettling the political landscape also in geographically removed Gulf countries such as Yemen and Bahrain to armed international intervention in Libya to oust Gaddafi to a full-fledged civil war in Syria. Within a few months, a region often conceived as a politically immutable space had experienced momentous transformations unseen since the fall of the Berlin Wall.[3]

In the case of the Egyptian revolution, several accounts provided first-hand narratives of the 18 days of demonstrations leading to the downfall of Hosni Mubarak, focusing on various issues such as the changing social geography of Cairo, the reactions of demonstrators recorded in the social media or through more traditional means, as well as the choreography

DOI: 10.1057/9781137395924

and aesthetics of protests.[4] On the other hand, another strand of literature has attempted to recast the Egyptian revolution within a longer and broader perspective, discussing the evolution of state, regime and society and their interrelations with the aim of shedding light on deeper factors that might have contributed to the uprisings. While paying attention also to the more contingent aspects, particularly in the latter chapters, this work principally aims to contribute to this second strand trying to cast the events of January and February 2011 in a longer-term perspective.

More generally, whereas all of these accounts clearly provide something valuable for our understanding of the revolts leading to the fall of Mubarak, it appears that most of the emerging literature is limited by either of three weaknesses, which this study seeks to overcome. Firstly, in much of the work produced particularly by Western think tanks but on occasions also by Arab observers (Osman 2011), there appears to be an inherent bias in favour of liberal democracy. Whereas certainly *horreya* (freedom) and *dimuqratya* (democracy) were among the main slogans chanted in the squares of the main Egyptian cities, this does not in itself justify the exclusive focus on the authoritarian character of the regime. As discussed later on, '*adala igtimaya* (social justice) was an equally powerful motto, and one that recalls the importance of distribution and redistribution of wealth and power, somewhat overlooked by liberal democratic perspectives. Indeed, whereas authoritarianism was certainly the main concern for the aspirational middle classes with the economic means to rely less and less on the state, for large strata of Egyptian society the main concern was exactly the lack of economic means. This assertion is easily backed by the replacement of welfare provision with forms of private support for the poor, as demonstrated by the ever more common practice of electoral bribes exposed by Samer Soliman (2011), and effectively underpinning the rise to political office of several businessmen. In this respect, it helps to refer back to Ray Hinnebusch (2006), who had argued that *exactly* because of the limited participation to political life, authoritarian regimes have to rely even more on good economic performance and on the payment of side benefits in order to keep their population, and particularly the lower classes, if not supportive to the regime at least acquiescent to the status quo. This dimension of the political economy of authoritarianism in the Middle East is one that accounts such as the one by Osman fail to take adequately into account.

Secondly, there is a tendency on the part of several accounts to focus on what are at best proximal causes of the Egyptian revolution, thus

DOI: 10.1057/9781137395924

somehow neglecting deeper and longer-term transformations in the economy and in society. This tendency has taken two main forms. On the one hand, different accounts tend to focus on the pivotal role of new technologies in the Arab Spring as a whole, which has produced a 'Revolution 2.0', as Wael Ghonim put it (2012). The argument here is that the penetration of information society in the Middle East, particularly in the form of social media such as Twitter and Facebook, has substantially transformed the dynamics of political activism and mobilisation, creating a new ground where dissent could be expressed and organised, and a ground that was much less amenable to regime control. Now, whereas it is undeniable that these new forms of communication have certainly facilitated the organisation of various forms of dissent, one should not forget two important elements. The first is the very limited penetration of internet outside of the main urban centres. A quick glance at the 2010 ICT Development Report by the United Nations telecoms agency tells us that only about 3 per cent of rural households had internet access by 2008. The second is that the immediate reaction of the regime to the demonstrations started on 25 January was to shut down the internet for five days. While this certainly suggests a growing fear of the power of new technologies on the part of the regime, it should also lead us to believe that more conventional forms of organisation on the ground need to be taken into adequate account for understanding the resilience of protestors, and indeed their increase in size and strength, despite the internet shutdown.

On the other hand, several authors have focussed on the interaction of structural demographic pressures with economic contingency, characterised by the impact of the global food and financial crises in the region. The interaction of these factors led to the sudden and dramatic increase in youth unemployment, particularly for the more educated. At the end of the day, the spark setting off the Arab Spring was the self-immolation of an unemployed graduate who set himself to fire as he was harassed by police forces for selling vegetables without a licence on the streets of Sidi Bouzid. Again, the discontent of a jobless generation is certainly to be factored into any explanation of the Arab uprisings. At the same time, finding its roots in a sudden deterioration of economic conditions mostly due to exogenous factors is grossly misleading, as it furthers the mistaken perception of an immutable Middle East, and thus discourages the undertaking of a longer-term analysis of the deeper transformations taking place in the region. In other words, both the financial and food

DOI: 10.1057/9781137395924

crises and the transformations in communication technologies are better interpreted as triggers of the Egyptian revolution rather than as root causes. Thus, they help us greatly in providing informed answers to the crucial question relating to the 'when' of the revolution. While the final chapters of the book do take stock of the many precious insights contained in these accounts, the question that the bulk of this book primarily seeks to address concerns the 'why' of the Egyptian revolution. And I maintain that understanding this requires digging deeper into the economic, political, social and cultural transformations that Egypt experienced in the two decades preceding 25 January 2011.

Thirdly, in the literature framing the Egyptian revolution within a broader historical process, there is a tendency either to pay insufficient attention to socio-economic dynamics, or to interpret them exclusively under the light of cronyism and corruption.[5] This is obviously a crucial dimension of the functioning of the Egyptian political economy, and indeed the durability of patron-client, nepotistic and outright corrupt forms of economic and political interaction is given due attention in Chapter 3. Once more, however, focusing only on these continuities provides a one-sided picture of the causes of the revolution, and one that fits extremely well with the liberal democratic mainstream narrative, which tends to pin down increased socio-economic inequality exactly to the persistence of shady practices that tend to limit opportunities for most of the Egyptians. The corollary of this view is that only reforms opening the economy to market forces would break down the prevalence of these practices by showing their inefficiency (Schlumberger 2008; Wurzel 2009). However, what these perspectives tend to miss is that market forces have already made significant strides in the Egyptian economy, effectively also leading to an adaptation of those very practices of patronage that are criticised. Indeed, this study maintains that examining this interaction between 'differential integration' in the global political economy, as Fred Halliday put it (2002), and pre-existing practices is crucial for getting a more detailed picture of the political economy of the Egyptian revolution, as it allows to go beyond the apparent continuities and to reconcile them with the dramatic socio-economic transformations Egypt has seen since the late 1980s.

In order to grasp the magnitude of these transformations one has to go back to the keywords that rocked Tahrir Square. Here as well as in the squares of Alexandria, Suez, Port Said and most other Egyptian cities, the most popular slogan was undoubtedly *'eish, karama, 'adala igtimaya*.

DOI: 10.1057/9781137395924

Bread, dignity, social justice. And its popularity is certainly related to the fact that it expressed the most fundamental grievances underpinning the largest and most sustained protests that Egypt had experienced since the end of British colonial rule. Bread, its scarce supply and increasing prices despite persisting government subsidies, was what had pushed the supposedly apathetic and a-political urban poor to take to the street and demand what had happened to the promise of higher living standards on which wide-ranging economic reforms had been based. Dignity was what most Egyptians felt deprived of, to the point of creating a united front – secularists and religious, Christians and Muslims, socialists and liberals – with the common aim of 'restor[ing] the meaning of politics' (El-Ghobashi 2011). Social justice had also sank into oblivion, as the privatisation and liberalisation of the economy had led to widening opportunities for very few, who exploited them towards an unprecedented concentration of wealth and power in their own hands, matched by a staggering increase in both real and perceived inequality.

As discussed by Galal Amin (2011), inequality increased constantly since the early 1990s and at accelerated pace since 2004. Ironically enough, the years between 1991 and 1996 and between 2004 and 2009 were the ones in which Egyptian policy-makers were repeatedly praised by international financial institutions (IFIs) and main donors for their efforts in reforming the national economy. Given this striking dissonance between the perception of successful economic reforms on the part of external actors and increasing social tension within the country, this book seeks to explore the nature of these reforms, in both the proposed and implemented versions, and whether their distributional impact might have had polarising consequences. This is done by looking on the one hand at how economic reforms have changed the relations of force within the different social groups supporting the Mubarak regime, and on the other hand at how increasing inequality has hit not only the lower classes, and thus industrial workers, peasants and informal labourers, but also most sections of the Egyptian middle class, pauperised by those very reforms that were meant to bolster its own position within society.

In other words, the argument that this book advances is that neoliberal reforms promoted by the IMF and the World Bank and implemented by the various governments since the early 1990s provided a fundamental precondition for the collapse of the authoritarian regime led by Hosni Mubarak. However, this did not happen – as reform supporters would have it – through the creation of a strong and independent middle

DOI: 10.1057/9781137395924

class that turned against a repressive regime, but rather by squeezing those very social groups historically constituting the middle class, and effectively pushing them towards the working classes, both in terms of income and discontent. At the same time, these reforms also alienated to the emerging new business class the sympathies of the two other main constituencies that had historically supported the regime: the army and the public sector. Thus, contrary to what modernisation and democratisation theory hold, it was not affluence and independence from the state to drive the call for an end to authoritarian rule. Rather, it was increasing deprivation. And desperation.

Arguments and evidence: notes on research design, methods and sources

What existing accounts have certainly grasped, and what was clearly on display, was a wave of popular mobilisation that in a few weeks had disproved decades of writings on the supposed passivity of the Egyptian population. The ability on the part of the people to reclaim power in all its key dimensions, particularly visible in the very occupation of previously heavily controlled and militarised spaces such as Tahrir Square, has recently inspired some excellent scholarly work (Tripp 2012). At the same time, particularly in authoritarian regimes where power is by definition concentrated in the hands of a restricted number of actors, the study of these transformations requires also to understand how the carefully constructed balance between different groups supporting the regime might have been upset by economic reforms. In other words, if the focus on middle and lower classes allows us to understand the demands of the revolution, one should primarily look at decision-makers to understand why bread was lacking, dignity was humiliated and social justice forgotten. Thus, this book starts from analysing the nature of the economic reforms proposed and implemented, before addressing the crucial question of their distributional impact both on the different social groups supporting the Mubarak regime and on the main social classes, and fractions thereof. Looking at these aspects, this work aims to uncover the socio-economic preconditions that created and bred discontent in large swathes of Egyptian society.

The nature of Egypt as a case study within this specific research project is twofold. On the one hand, one of the key arguments of this

DOI: 10.1057/9781137395924

work is that the economic reforms implemented in the 1990s and 2000s have transformed the Egyptian economy along neoliberal lines. In this respect, Egypt is best considered as a least-likely case for neoliberalism to succeed. As this point is still subject to contestation within the specialist literature, showing that the Egyptian political economy has been significantly neoliberalised already constitutes an important contribution in its own right. On the other hand, this study also attempts to establish a novel account of the relation between economic and political transformations using the Egyptian case as a plausibility probe.

The argument that Egypt is a least-likely case for neoliberalism to succeed rests on three conditions characterising the Egyptian political economy in the late 1980s that are usually considered hostile to neoliberal pressures. Firstly, since the Camp David agreement of 1977 Egypt had come to play a pivotal role in the US strategy in the Middle East. As a consequence of this, it had been allowed to indulge in the politics of 'dilatory reform' for most of the 1980s (Richards 1991), exactly because its fundamental strategic position had been used skilfully in international negotiating fora to postpone reforms and keep foreign aid flowing into the country. At the same time, this peculiarity also meant that foreign direct investment (FDI) had historically had a marginal role in the economy of republican Egypt.

Secondly, by the end of the 1980s the regime of capital accumulation in Egypt was far away from the neoliberal regime that had become prevalent in many developed and developing countries. Indeed, in the 1960s Egypt was arguably the country that got closest to the communist bloc with respect to state intervention and direct participation in the economy. In this respect, whereas the *infitah* (opening) carried out by Sadat sought to reverse this situation, it only marginally succeeded in doing so, particularly as the economy became increasingly reliant on various forms of rent. By the end of the 1980s, the state was still by far the largest actor in the economy, seemingly discouraging the adoption of policies starting from the assumption that the state was the main economic problem.

Thirdly, both material conditions and ideas did not seem particularly propitious. On the one hand, the predominant role of the state in the economy reverberated on the social structure, as the state was effectively able to create its own classes, as it happened first with the state bourgeoisie in the 1960s, largely composed of bureaucrats, technocrats and army members (Hinnebusch 1985), and then with the *infitah* bourgeoisie in the 1970s, which despite being private and formally independent still

DOI: 10.1057/9781137395924

heavily relied on the state for its prosperity. On the other hand, economic nationalism had been the main ideology among Egyptian elites even before 1952 (Vitalis 1995; Ezzel Arab 2002), and also in this respect the *infitah* had fallen short of producing a change in the economic policy discourse.

Other than providing conditions generally hostile to neoliberalism, the Egyptian case also presents a difficult puzzle for mainstream explanations. Modernisation and democratisation theory, for example, suggest that reforms aiming at opening up the economy provide the conditions for the development of a strong and autonomous middle class that would in turn push for political opening. In Egypt, it appears that exactly this type of reform weakened, if anything, the local middle class, and on the other hand allowed the rise of a capitalist oligarchy with little or no interest in moving beyond authoritarian rule. Accounts based on the predatory elite thesis also encounter similar difficulties. Their key prediction is that rent-based behaviours typical of elites in authoritarian contexts neutralise any substantial restructuring of politico-economic relations, with the political logic of power maintenance taking precedence over the logic of economic efficiency. Yet, the Egyptian case suggests that reforms went beyond this point, in the direction of a more thorough restructuring of social relations. Thus, studying Egypt forces us to go beyond these mainstream explanations that appear inadequate to grasp the magnitude and direction of the changes experienced by the Egyptian political economy.

Given these limitations of mainstream explanations, this study develops and assesses the potential of an alternative approach, inspired by the insights of the Italian Marxist Antonio Gramsci. While this account holds in the face of the evidence gathered with respect to the Egyptian case, its potential for becoming a more general theory would have to be evaluated in the light of other case studies (Odell 2001). However, as suggested in much literature on the theoretical value of plausibility probes (George and Bennett 2005; Levy 2008), this is not necessarily a problem. Indeed, as long as the standards of rigour with respect to both the translation of concepts into reliable empirical referents and the methods for gathering and analysing evidence are not lowered, plausibility probes can provide a fruitful way of addressing existing gaps in the literature from novel theoretical perspectives.

These different yet interrelated research objectives are best achieved through a form of methodological pluralism combining qualitative research methods with the use of descriptive statistics. The latter play

DOI: 10.1057/9781137395924

a fundamental role for discussing the narrative of Egypt as a successful reformer as portrayed by the IMF and the World Bank in the past decade and pit it against the thesis of the neoliberalisation of the Egyptian economy advanced in this study. More specifically, aggregate data from sources ranging from the World Bank's World Development Indicators (WDI) to the Central Bank of Egypt (CBE) to the Ministry of Finance are employed to show the degree to which processes of privatisation and financialisation occurred in Egypt in the past two decades. Descriptive statistics on a more disaggregate level are equally helpful in providing an idea of the spectacular rise in the wealth of a few business conglomerates, some with origins in the *infitah* era and others whose emergence is more directly related to the reforms examined here.

Among qualitative methods, process-tracing plays a fundamental role. On the one hand, a documented discussion of the different steps in the causal path hypothesised by both democratisation and predatory elite theories provides the chance to understand more specifically their limits in accounting for the Egyptian case. On the other hand, through process-tracing it is also possible to evaluate the alternative causal path proposed from neoliberal economic reforms to an increase in inequality and polarisation in Egyptian society to a gradual erosion of consent for the regime responsible for the approval and implementation of those very reforms. These different steps in the causal chain are assessed through reliance on secondary sources, but most importantly through first-hand empirical research conducted during two stays in Cairo, respectively between March and July 2010 and between June and July 2013. Among the former, the two most important English-language outlets for information about the Egyptian economy – namely the Economist Intelligence Unit (EIU) reports and the Middle East Economic Digest (MEED) – have been used extensively to contextualise material emerging from first-hand empirical research. This has taken two main forms.

Firstly, reports issued by IFIs as well as the actual reform bills passed by the Egyptian parliament have been analysed in order to grasp on the one hand the similarities and differences between proposed and implemented reforms, and on the other hand the degree to which policy change occurred and whether the shift amounted to a paradigm change (Hall 1993). Similarly, the policy-oriented production on the part of the two most important economic think tanks in the country – the Economic Research Forum (ERF) and the Egyptian Center for Economic Studies (ECES) – has been analysed with the aim of assessing the degree of

DOI: 10.1057/9781137395924

norm internalisation and the emergence of cognitive biases with respect to economic policies.

Secondly, 18 semi-structured interviews were conducted in order to grasp the details of negotiations between national and international institutions. The national institutions targeted were the Ministry of Investment, the Ministry of Finance, the Ministry of Trade and Industry, the Central Bank of Egypt and the Egyptian Exchange (EGX). As suggested by the prologue above, persistence combined with rather fortunate circumstances allowed me to get direct access to top policy-makers. This once more provided the opportunity to evaluate how neoliberal economic principles were used in order to frame changes in economic policy, while at the same time also trying to understand something more on the emerging rifts within the ruling coalition. In the attempt of grasping the diffusion of these ideas, interviews were not exclusively targeted at key policy-makers, but rather at officials at various levels of seniority in the above institutions. Indeed, starting from the identification of people with an important role in the negotiation and/or implementation of reforms, a snowball sampling strategy has been used. Among international institutions, most interviewees belonged to the EU delegation to Egypt, the US Agency for International Development (USAID) and the World Bank. Discussions with these officials were particularly helpful in identifying instances of cooperation, but also of diluted or delayed implementation and on some occasions of outright confrontation. All the material gathered from these interviews was further enriched by unstructured interviews carried out with other experts, either working in economic think tanks or in economics departments in Egyptian universities.

With respect to the timeframe, this study focuses primarily on the two decades between 1991 and 2010. The year 1991 represents a key year because that was when the Egyptian government signed the Economic Reform and Structural Adjustment Programme (ERSAP) with the IMF and the World Bank, which would become the first agreement with IFIs that Egypt would carry out until its completion. On the other hand of the timeframe, most of the empirical research was conducted in Cairo in the year before Mubarak's overthrow. However, while mostly focusing on these two decades, the evidence gathered, particularly as it has been improved upon during the recent stay in Egypt, also sheds some light on the political economy of the first post-Mubarak years, up until the removal of Mohamed Morsi in July 2013.

DOI: 10.1057/9781137395924

Argument in a nutshell and outline

So, going back to Mohieldin, what was different this time and why? Until the late 1980s reform efforts in Egypt had been aimed at provisionally improving the financial position of the state before reverting to the same old policies and practices. Departing from this pattern, reforms undertaken since the early 1990s fundamentally altered the Egyptian political economy. This transformation is best understood with reference to shifting relations of class forces within Egyptian society. Two shifts were particularly notable: on the one hand, within the ruling bloc, reforms empowered the outward-oriented private sector component *vis-à-vis* other sections of the ruling bloc, and most notably the hitherto dominant army; on the other hand, within society at large, such reforms led to runaway inequality, considerably increasing the distance between the ruling bloc and subaltern classes, now including most sections of the middle class and all of the working classes. These shifts had three significant implications for any remnants of hegemony on the national scale on the part of the Mubarak regime. It is argued that, firstly, the interaction between international organisations and national government led to the implementation of a neoliberal programme which was articulated with the pre-existing corporatist and patron-client practices in the attempt of 'domesticating' neoliberalism and containing its potentially disruptive effect on the regime. Secondly, the interaction of economic and political factors contributed greatly to the rise of a new business class and to its swift transformation into a capitalist oligarchy with visible predatory tendencies. This in turn created major tensions within the ruling bloc, further exacerbating the 'winner-take-all' tendencies of this emerging social group. Lastly, the performative power of neoliberalism as an ideology fundamentally reshaped the boundaries of economic policy-making in favour of large, outward-oriented, private Egyptian capital, but failed to provide the basis for the emergence of a broader coalition supporting this shift. All these developments suggest that the main domestic sources of state hegemony in Egypt dried up over the past two decades, and that the shift to a neoliberal accumulation regime, and its articulation with pre-existing practices, appears to be the main reason for this.

In the attempt to substantiate this argument, this work proceeds in the following way. Chapter 1 identifies the common thread underlying Gramsci's writings in the 'philosophy of praxis', best understood as a form of historical dialectical materialism. The most distinctive theoretical and

DOI: 10.1057/9781137395924

methodological insight deriving from this is the concept of articulation, which allows us to understand in a dynamic form the constitution, reproduction, transformation and unravelling of hegemony. The focus on articulation serves not the scope of developing an alternative Gramscian *theory*, but rather to suggest how Gramsci can provide the foundations of an alternative *method* for studying continuities and transformations in the global political economy. In empirical terms, articulation is particularly useful when adopted to study the three different instances of the relation between structure and superstructure at the heart of Gramsci's thought, encompassing respectively the international and the national, the economic and the political, the material and the ideational. In other words, the articulation approach developed here allows us to bring respectively the national, the political and the ideational back in, eschewing globalist, economistic and vulgar materialist tendencies, while at the same time retaining a focus on social relations between classes and fractions thereof.

The following three chapters discuss in much greater detail the three forms of articulation outlined in Chapter 1. Chapter 2 thus moves along the international–national dimension. This means looking at the different rounds of negotiations between the IMF and the World Bank and the Egyptian government, in the attempt of understanding what concessions and exemptions were extracted by national actors with respect to the reforms they were required to adopt, and whether these concessions and exemptions fundamentally altered the nature of the reform project as a whole. The main argument emerging from this analysis is that the global logic of neoliberal capital accumulation promoted by IFIs was articulated with a national logic of gradual reform and development, best summarised by Mohieldin's claim that 'Egypt is no country for shock therapy'. Thus, the government was significantly able to influence the timing, sequencing and increasingly also the content of reforms.

Chapter 3 instead focuses on the distributional consequences of the reforms adopted, thus analysing the interaction of wealth and power, of economic and political factors. This puts us in the condition to identify the main winners and losers of the process of neoliberalisation, both within and outside the regime. The analysis of the political economy of reforms allows us to track down the routes by which a handful of business groups, some of them belonging to the *infitah* bourgeoisie and some emerging anew, managed to amass an unprecedented amount of wealth. In particular, the new business class attempted to and succeeded

DOI: 10.1057/9781137395924

in translating its growing economic influence into direct political power, which was deployed towards the reorganisation of authoritarian rule under a different accumulation regime.

The interaction of material and ideational factors in the rise of neoliberalism as a new policy and discursive paradigm within the new business class is at the heart of Chapter 4. The main argument advanced here is that the role of economic ideas is best understood if these are situated socially, and more specifically if they are related to the classes and class fractions who support/oppose and/or are empowered/weakened by them. At the same time, it is suggested that once settled within a given social setting, ideas might actually take a life of their own, eventually contributing to reshaping those material conditions from which they originated. Empirically, the chapter focuses on creation of the two most important economic think tanks in Egypt respectively on the part of international organisations and donors and on the part of the new business class. Their role as organic intellectuals providing a credible and relatively coherent platform for the rising class fraction is discussed with reference to their scientific production, and more specifically their working paper series. At the same time, the neoliberal economic discourse was articulated with a political discourse that put a strong emphasis on regime stability, in order not to appear threatening to other components of the ruling bloc. Despite these attempts, neoliberal ideas as articulated by the new business class failed in winning the support of most other sections of Egyptian society, thus proving themselves incapable of providing the basis for a renewed hegemony on the national scale.

The consequences that evolutions on these three forms of articulation had on the strength and stability of state hegemony under Mubarak is assessed in the first part of Chapter 5. This provides the chance to identify with clarity the main long-term socio-economic determinants that had been transforming Egyptian society much more than most external observers were inclined to believe. These socio-economic trends are interpreted as the deeper causes (the 'why'), which were activated by the contingent processes and events on which much literature has focused, ranging from the global financial and food crisis to the penetration of new technologies to the emulation effect from Tunisia (the 'when').

Lastly, the conclusion pulls the threads together in order to highlight the main theoretical and empirical contributions of this work. It also tries to understand whether ongoing political transformations are likely to produce also a change with respect to the Egyptian political economy.

DOI: 10.1057/9781137395924

The recent ousting of president Morsi might indeed signal a return to the *status quo ante*, with the army restoring its predominant position in a new version of the alliance with private capital, both domestic and foreign, this time cleansed from the elements more directly associated with Gamal Mubarak. Not everything appears to be lost though. Continuing mobilisation, on the streets and squares of Egyptian cities, in the spinning and weaving mills of the Delta and in the countryside, is likely to persist and act as a check on the moves of the newly appointed government if this does not respond to the original demands of the revolution. After all, as Fawaz Gerges put it, the exit of Mubarak 'removes the barrier of fear in the region' (2011). This is undoubtedly a consolidated result of the Egyptian revolution, and one which the army and its political allies would better keep in mind.

Notes

1   Interview with Mahmoud Mohieldin, then minister of investment, Cairo, 4 July 2010.
2   In light of the success of this self-definition, the term 'reformist' is used in this work to identify the faction of the Egyptian ruling bloc in favour of free market reforms.
3   Ironically, but for some unsurprisingly (Tetlock 2006), the fall of the Berlin Wall and the following collapse of the Soviet bloc provide an important precedent to the Arab uprisings in terms of highlighting the predictive failure of area specialists in foreseeing imminent transformations. On the case of Soviet collapse, see Cox (1999).
4   See, for example, Ashraf Khalil 2011, Karima Khalil 2011, Nuns and Idle 2011, Rushdy 2011, Soueif 2012.
5   The first tendency is evident for example in the already mentioned account by John Bradley (2008). The second can be encountered in the otherwise extremely helpful account of Egyptian socio-political history by Steven Cook (2012), and in the collection of articles by Alaa Al Aswany (2011), arguably the most prominent living Egyptian novelist.

DOI: 10.1057/9781137395924

1
A Gramscian Approach to the Study of the Political Economy of Reforms

Abstract: *This chapter establishes the rationale for developing an approach to the political economy of reforms based on Gramsci's thought. Particular emphasis is placed on the method of articulation, which provides a more reliable basis than that offered by existing neo-Gramscian approaches to the study of the constitution, consolidation, reproduction, transformation and at times crisis of hegemony in authoritarian contexts.*

Keywords: Gramsci; method of articulation; hegemony; neo-Gramscian IPE; neoliberalism

Roccu, Roberto. *The Political Economy of the Egyptian Revolution: Mubarak, Economic Reforms and Failed Hegemony.* Basingstoke: Palgrave Macmillan, 2014. DOI: 10.1057/9781137395924.

Since its introduction to International Relations (IR) and International Political Economy (IPE) in the early 1980s, Gramsci's writings have become an important reference point for scholars interested in bridging the analysis of economic structure and political and ideological superstructures. This common interest has led to a proliferation of neo-Gramscian approaches, with scholars relying on Gramsci to support arguments as disparate as the emergence of a global civil society (Lipschutz 1992), the prospects of a post-liberal democracy (Golding 1992) and the cultural turn in post-colonial theory and subaltern studies (Harris 1993). However, despite the positioning of his work right at the crux where the international and the national, the economic and the political, the material and the ideational meet, Gramsci has rarely been invoked to address the political economy of reforms in the developing world, and more specifically in the Middle East. This is unfortunate for two reasons. Firstly, Gramsci's work allows us to study the consequences of neoliberal economic reforms by still focusing on the conditioning power held by the economic structure and the relations of class forces underlying it, while at the same time avoiding the shallows of deterministic Marxist approaches (Germain and Kenny 1998). Secondly, the suitability of Gramsci's insights to the study of the political economy of the Middle East has been seriously underexploited. In the past decades, Gramsci has increasingly been called upon to discuss specific elements of the international relations of the Middle East, ranging from the US foreign policy towards Iraq and its relation to state autonomy (Dodge 2006), to the reproduction of cultures and identities in Egypt as an obstacle to meaningful democratisation (Pratt 2005). Despite these valuable contributions, to my knowledge the only systematic attempt to develop a Gramscian framework for analysing the political economy of the region came from Nazih Ayubi (1995). However, the explicit focus on the regional dimension of his study means that little attention was paid to the international dimension, both with respect to the globalising tendencies of capital accumulation and to the specific policies adopted by social groups and institutions active on the international scale. Yet, Gramsci's peculiar biography, with a childhood in then underdeveloped Sardinia followed by university studies in Turin, one of the outposts of European industrial capitalism in the early twentieth century, suggests that he might have something to tell us about how developed and developing countries interact with each other, and what are the social relations mobilised by these interactions.

DOI: 10.1057/9781137395924

Starting from these considerations, this chapter is organised in the following way. The first section discusses mainstream explanations of the relation between liberalising economic reforms and the impact they are expected to have on the political regime, in order to show where they fail in accounting for the political impact of economic reforms in the specific Egyptian case. The second section fleshes out the Gramscian approach adopted in this study, with specific emphasis on the use of articulation as a method for understanding the different dimensions on which hegemony is constructed, affirmed and consolidated, but also transformed, challenged and undermined. The final section discusses how the Gramscian method used here can be reconciled with a study that focuses mostly on Egyptian elites.

Why Gramsci? The limitations of mainstream approaches

The mainstream literature on the relation between economic reforms and regime change is composed of two broad traditions of thought that are often pitted against each other. The first one can be traced back to modernisation theory, with democratisation theory as its main offspring.[1] The second tradition instead focuses more specifically on the role of elites in authoritarian contexts and on how they tend to exploit the position within the existing regime in order to neutralise the potentially transformative impact of economic reforms. As discussed in this section, neither of these conceptual frameworks is able to account adequately for what has happened in Egypt. This is the first and foremost reason for looking beyond these established traditions in order to develop an alternative narrative of the political economy of reforms in Egypt.

According to modernisation and democratisation theory, there is a positive relationship between liberalising economic reforms and the chances of democratisation of the political regime. Being interested in explaining the conditions of successful economic development, in Rostow's seminal formulation modernisation theory did not have direct interest in the study of democracy and political regimes (1960). However, it is not difficult to read an argument between the lines. As economic development occurs, societies become functionally more complex and socially more mobilised, thus putting centralised forms of government increasingly under strain and increasing the likelihood of

DOI: 10.1057/9781137395924

more open political regimes. This argument is fleshed out more systematically within democratisation theory, and particularly in the work of Lipset (1959) and Huntington (1991). While Rostow's account erred on the structuralist side almost to the point of determinism, democratisation theory identifies the middle class as the key agent emerging from liberalising economic reforms and with an interest in opening up also the political regime. More specifically, there is a set of three interrelated claims emerging from this literature with respect to the relation between economic development, democratisation and the role of the middle class. Firstly, capitalist development leads to the emergence of a strong and autonomous middle class. Secondly, in virtue of being both strong and autonomous, the middle class has a strong interest in leading democratic transition. Thirdly, both in times of recession and rapid economic growth, as they both unsettle the existing order, economic opening is likely to improve the prospects of democratic transition.

Unfortunately, 'the middle class' as such remains undefined. Indeed, as Luciani put it (2007: 163), 'the middle class *per se* has no other distinguishing feature except that it finds itself between a top class, comprising the elites, and a lower class, comprising the masses'. If one is to take such a definition, then the middle class can become the main agent of democratisation because it has both the capabilities and the will to support democracy. This clearly does not happen for the upper and the lower class. The former might have the capabilities to support regime change, but being the main beneficiary of the current political arrangement it obviously lacks the will. The latter might want to change the state of affairs, but lacks the capabilities to do it.

Despite the *prima facie* validity of this account, breaking down the middle class in its various components shows immediately that its composition varies greatly from case to case. In advanced democracies, the crucial case study for Lipset, the middle class is mostly composed of small and medium entrepreneurs, self-employed professionals and private sector employees, with the public sector constituting a relative minority. In the case of Brazil, on which Huntington insists, at the time of transition the middle class was mostly composed of medium-size entrepreneurs and private sector employees, with a sizeable yet not overwhelming public sector (Martins 1986; Cardoso 1986). In Middle Eastern post-populist countries, with Egypt being the most prominent among them, public sector employees constitute the bulk of the middle class, with small and medium entrepreneurs and self-employed professionals

DOI: 10.1057/9781137395924

having a limited weight. Following from this, the structure of incentives and opportunities with respect to democratic transition may change considerably.

Most importantly, if one is to look at how the economic reforms implemented in Egypt since the late 1980s, clearly informed by neoliberal principles, impacted on these different sections of the middle class the causal chain hypothesised by modernisation and democratisation theory breaks down. Despite limited data availability, in this respect it is reasonable to assume that professions were able to hold their ground, and on occasions even improve their relative position, in the past two decades. This has most likely left self-employed professionals with enough resources, mostly earned outside of the regime circuit, to be mobilised in the political sphere. Thus, traditional modernisation and democratisation theory are proven right in this respect and the emergence of middle class protest movements such as *Kefaya* (Enough) already in 2005 further witnesses this. At the same time, the largest component of the middle class was significantly squeezed by these reforms. Public sector employees have seen their real wages deteriorating substantially (Said 2009), and have increasingly resorted to moonlighting and the informal labour market to cope with financial difficulties (Moktar and Wahba 2002; Wahba 2009). Thus, it is difficult to maintain that their participation in the 25 January protests is due to increased affluence and independence from the regime. On the aggregate level, as discussed in the following chapters, economic reforms produced a significant increase in inequality, with the emergence of a new business class whose wealth is comparable to those of the Western super-rich and the impoverishment of large sections of the middle class and virtually all of the working class. In other words, if liberalising economic reforms were meant to bolster the middle class and push it to support democratisation, then modernisation and democratisation theory are only able to account for a small section of the middle class, and we need to seek for a better explanation for Mubarak's fall.

Accounts based on the predatory elite thesis, on the other hand, suggest that rent-based behaviours typical of elites in authoritarian contexts act as an effective guardian of the regime, appropriating most of the benefits deriving from reforms and neutralising any substantial restructuring of political relations. In other words, the political logic of power maintenance is said to take precedence over the logic of economic efficiency.[2] Regardless of whether elites are conceptualised as distributional coalitions or informal networks,[3] the common assumptions of

DOI: 10.1057/9781137395924

these accounts are that in authoritarian contexts actions by members of the elites influence outcomes disproportionately more than actions by non-elite members and that these actions are based on considerations of self-interest and welfare maximisation. Following from these assumptions, and given the positional advantage that elites enjoy by definition, rent-seeking becomes the way by which they can attempt to consolidate their position within the reformed economic system. Thus, the basic argument here is that new economic policies do not have a systemic impact on the political regime, but at best force well-positioned actors to adapt their behaviour so that they can maintain and whenever possible consolidate their privileged position. Through these processes of adaptation and consolidation, spill-overs in the political sphere would then be avoided.

The significant room enjoyed by well-placed political agents in shaping to a good extent the final outcomes of the reform process is what these accounts are best able to account for. As we will see in Chapter 3, the correlation between being a member of the *infitah* bourgeoisie in 1990 and being one of the main beneficiaries of the reform process is quite neat. Those that did not belong to that section of the private sector and yet made it into the ruling bloc over the past two decades did so by forging alliances with members of the regime, and often through personal friendships, for example with the president's son Gamal. In Egypt, politics is a key factor in determining the effect of economic reforms on your position in the social structure, and accounts focusing on rent-seeking elites account for this aspect remarkably well.

However, these accounts suffer from two major deficiencies which suggest that the quest for an alternative approach be undertaken. Firstly, there is a tendency to apply the concept of rent in an undifferentiated way over the entire ruling group, at times entirely falling under the predatory category (Levi 1988). Following from this, it becomes difficult to account for the evolution of relations *within* the ruling bloc. In the specific Egyptian case, these approaches tend to overestimate the role of intra-regime alliances between potential winners and losers acting as a veto that either stifles or derails the reform impetus (Kienle 2001 and 2003; Wurzel 2009), while systematically overlooking deepening fractures between the different components of the ruling bloc, which are discussed at length in the following chapters. Secondly, the exclusive focus on elites produces a very damaging neglect, from an analytical perspective, of the unintended consequences that economic reforms

DOI: 10.1057/9781137395924

can have on society at large. In Egypt, these are visible once again in the impoverishment of middle and lower classes, and the increasing gap with the 5 per cent of the population holding more than 40 per cent of the country's wealth (Osman 2010: 115).

As both modernisation theory and elite-centred accounts tend to underestimate the nuances of the differentiated impact that economic reforms have had both within the ruling bloc and in broader society, it is worthwhile to turn our attention to a theoretical tradition that instead has made of his attention to social groups, usually defined in terms of classes, one of its main points of strength. Within the Marxist fold, referring more specifically to Gramsci allows us to look at the material impact of economic reforms on social classes without forsaking the way in which superstructures, among which regime type, do have a significant influence with respect to which reforms are adopted, in which way and for the intended benefit of whom. However, the IPE literature inspired by Gramsci very seldom ventures outside of the comfort zone of the developed world, focusing mostly on issues concerning US hegemony or the emergence of a transnational capitalist class.[4] Whenever the developing or underdeveloped world is touched upon from this perspective, these approaches tend to fall back towards a form of Western-centric diffusionism, with actors on the national scale in developing countries largely seen as void of political agency. Following from this, the analysis tends to overemphasise the coherence of global or transnational hegemonic projects. However, the Egyptian case suggests that the national scale, both with respect to its ruling bloc and to broader society, does have a significant role in articulating external pressures and trying to bend them to pursue genuinely domestic goals.

There are also significant exceptions already within existing neo-Gramscian approaches, with more and more studies focusing on the developing world and exposing the 'travelling problem' of the dominant interpretations by Robert Cox on the one hand and Kees Van der Pijl on the other hand.[5] Adam Morton (2007 and 2011) is arguably the scholar who has gone further in developing a new understanding of Gramsci that does without the Eurocentrism characterising the first generation of neo-Gramscian studies. Taking Morton's work as a fundamental reference point, but also departing from it in some significant respects, the next section presents a novel approach to the study of the political economy of reforms in developing countries, which relies on one of the most pivotal yet hitherto neglected concepts in Gramsci's thinking,

DOI: 10.1057/9781137395924

that of 'philosophy of praxis', and the method of articulation that stems thereof.

Which Gramsci? Philosophy of praxis and the method of articulation

It is plausible to assume that 'philosophy of praxis' was used as a surrogate for historical materialism and Marxism in the first *Prison Notebooks*, in order to mislead suspicious yet not particularly well-read censors. However, as time went by and notes became more elaborate, one can see how this concept starts to take a life of its own and be charged with peculiar elements, beyond – and sometimes away from – classical historical materialism as developed by Marx and Engels. Thus, the phrase 'philosophy of praxis' is 'an accurate characterisation of his theoretical perspective as part of a long-standing tradition opposed to positivist, naturalist and scientific deformations of Marxism' (Piccone 1976: 37). And indeed, already in its own semantics this expression is an attack against mechanistic versions of Marxism, in that – by referring to praxis – Gramsci emphasises the importance of agency and of the strategies that political actors devise in order to achieve what they wish for. In much the same way, by linking philosophy to praxis, it is also an attack on speculative forms of idealism, that divorce theory from practice, leading to 'a mutilation of Hegelism and the dialectic' (Gramsci 1975: 1220).

In the mature Gramscian formulation, the philosophy of praxis is better understood as a form of *historical dialectical materialism*.[6] The first term refers to Gramsci's conception of history as both necessity and contingency. This importance of history and the way we approach it is crucial because, in his own words, '[i]t has been forgotten that in the case of a very common expression [historical materialism] one should put the accent on the first term – "historical" – and not on the second, which is of metaphysical origin. The philosophy of praxis is absolute "historicism", the absolute secularisation and earthliness of thought, an absolute humanism of history' (1971: 465). History is first of all defined as a progressive process, thereby implying some line of immanent development of events. This understanding carries an inherent tendency towards determinism, which is eschewed by treating history also as contingency, that is: a conjuncture with its own unique parameters, in economic, political and ideological terms, and therefore necessarily open-ended. It

DOI: 10.1057/9781137395924

is in this dialectical treatment of history that Gramsci's philosophy of praxis starts to take shape.

Gramsci's conception of the dialectic is the second element implied by the above characterisation of philosophy of praxis. Gramsci himself defined the dialectic as 'a doctrine of knowledge and the very marrow of historiography and the science of politics' (1971: 435). Despite such a strong claim, the role of this concept in Gramsci's thought has only received scant attention, with Bobbio's 1958 article still standing out as arguably the best treatment of the dialectic in Gramsci. In the *Prison Notebooks*, Gramsci develops a two-dimensional conception of the dialectic. On the one hand, Gramsci uses the dialectic in the classical understanding by Engels of compenetration of the opposites, thus allowing the philosophy of praxis to be both philosophy and praxis, establishing an interactive and mutually constitutive relation between theory and practice. This aspect emerges very clearly in Gramsci's critique of Benedetto Croce, undoubtedly the most prominent Hegelian philosopher in early twentieth-century Italy. On the other hand, the dialectic is also intended in the Hegelian definition as a process of thesis–antithesis–synthesis. Gramsci's critique of Bukharin is fundamental for understanding the relevance of this second dimension of the dialectic. In his *Historical Materialism*, Bukharin posits a distinction between the general and the particular, between what he calls Marxist philosophy and Marxist sociology, and decides to focus more specifically on the latter. Gramsci suggests that this way of proceeding produces a popularisation of historical materialism, but this happens through an unacceptable simplification of its complexity, and not by raising the cultural level of the subaltern groups. Indeed, the conception of the dialectic as thesis–antithesis–synthesis is forsaken with a slip into vulgar and mechanistic materialism, a closed system where agency is powerless in the face of an almighty structure (1975: 1422–1426). Thus, Croce is criticised for using the dialectic *à la* Hegel only, and Bukharin for using it exclusively *à la* Engels. Gramsci instead maintains that both these dimensions of the dialectic are integral to the philosophy of praxis.

Lastly, the philosophy of praxis also entails a peculiar understanding of materialism. In the critique of Croce and Bukharin briefly outlined above, Gramsci is not attacking idealism or materialism *per se*. The English editors of the *Selection from the Prison Notebooks* are in my view correct when they argue that Gramsci 'located the enemy of the philosophy of praxis not in idealism as such but in transcendence and metaphysics' (Hoare and Nowell Smith 1971: 378). Similarly, it is the mechanistic tendency of Bukharin's approach to be criticised, and not materialism as a whole. Thus, it is the goal of the philosophy of praxis to provide a new synthesis of materialism and idealism, under the aegis of a two-dimensional conception of the dialectic, which also allows us to consider history and practice as open-ended combinations of necessity and contingency, where also ideas and practices from the past can be re-actualised, and prove themselves useful beyond their original context.

At the same time, together with the understanding that the outcomes of the dialectic are perennially provisional, Gramsci also shows an acute awareness of those occasions in which the dialectical process does not produce a synthesis or an overcoming, but rather a juxtaposition of the different forces at play, be they material or ideational. For this reason, it makes sense to refer to the concept of *articulation*, which does not imply as strong a sense of progressive development as does the dialectic. Interestingly enough, articulation has received most attention in post-Marxist scholarship.[7] For instance, Laclau and Mouffe define articulation as 'any practice establishing a relation among elements such that their identity is modified as a result of the articulatory practice' (2001: 105). In the attempt of breaking away from the emphasis on necessity typical of the Third International, Laclau and Mouffe rely on articulation in order to redefine hegemony in what is allegedly a non-reductionist form. As a result, this displacement of hegemony beyond the ground of the social relations of production opens up the political space to a potentially infinite number of alternative articulations, creating a 'general field of discursivity' where hegemony is continually shaped and reshaped through antagonistic practices (2001: 135–136). As Morton puts it, this reading reduced Gramsci's key concepts such as hegemony and historical bloc to 'undefined social and political spaces that are unified by discursive formations within an irreducible pluralism' (2005: 442). At the end of the day, their position is much more similar than they would be willing to admit to that of Benedetto Croce, significantly characterised by Hobsbawm as 'the first post-Marxist' (1987: 268).

While moving away from the 'symptomatic' reading provided by Laclau and Mouffe, *articulation as a method* is of vital importance for understanding how the specific configuration taken by hegemony – the other key Gramscian concept – is shaped by the mutual interaction between structure and superstructure. The workings of articulation are best encapsulated in the concept of *historical bloc*, intended as a form of

DOI: 10.1057/9781137395924

asymmetrical yet mutual constitution. On the one hand, the term 'bloc' refers to the classical Marxist relation between the realm of production and the realm of state–civil society relations, with its political and ideological implications. On the other hand, the term 'historical' refers to the contingent conditions which define the specificities of any given relation between structure and superstructure, and thus the form taken by the historical bloc. These specificities are more often than not fought over and contested at the level of superstructures, yet they do have an impact on structures as such. In other words, this asymmetrical yet dialectical relation corresponds to a form of 'determinism in the first instance' as understood by Stuart Hall (1996: 45). From this perspective, the structure is seen as a first moulding influence defining what Braudel called the 'limits of the possible', thus setting the boundaries of a playing field within which political agency develops its strategies and projects. Following from this, a hegemonic project cannot be successful if it does not relate in some way to an existing or prospective economic strategy (Jessop 1990). At the same time, the relative autonomy enjoyed by superstructures means that in their interactions with the structure they manage to feed back on it and thus reshape those very boundaries within which agency works. This is displayed most clearly in Gramsci's remarks about the political nature of *laissez-faire* policies and yet their ability at the same time to reshape the economic structure and affect the distribution of wealth within a state (1971: 159–162).

For the sake of analytical clarity, and following a distinction which is mostly left implicit in the *Notebooks*, in this study the relation between structure and superstructure is disaggregated into three fundamental instances, in order to better grasp the different forms of articulation on which hegemony is constituted, reproduced, transformed and contested. Firstly, in the next chapter the focus is on the articulation between the international and the national scale. Hegemony emerges as an essentially national phenomenon, but its conditions of existence – and interscalar extension, whenever possible – are determined in the first instance by the international scale, and by the patterns of uneven and combined development characteristic of capitalist relations of production. A couple of brief examples from the history of republican Egypt may help to illustrate this mechanism. On the one hand, Nasser's attempt to develop hegemony at the national scale and extend it at the regional scale was certainly influenced by the climate of those years, but it was largely framed in opposition to both the post-war *Pax Americana* and the coercion-

DOI: 10.1057/9781137395924

intensive domination of the Soviet bloc by the USSR. On the other hand, the move away from Nasserist principles and the attempt to reconstruct hegemony on new foundations saw both Sadat and Mubarak trying to articulate the national scale along the lines advocated by the emerging form of neoliberal capitalism in the most developed economies.

Secondly, the attention shifts to the articulation of the economic and the political, which leads to a conception of hegemony which is inescapably linked to social relations of production, but is at the same time shaped by the struggle of social forces in the political arena. Again, Egyptian history provides a good example. Up until the late 1960s, Egypt pursued a state capitalist model, with an economic system revolving around the central role of the state. While responding to shifting global imperatives, Sadat's *infitah* also provided the state with the opportunity of creating its own capitalist class. In turn, this exercise of relative autonomy on the part of the state fed back on the economic structure, producing a restructuring of social relations of production.

Thirdly, the articulation between material and ideational factors is also analysed, highlighting how the discursive construction of hegemony is always intertwined with a material dimension of exchange, constituted for instance of side payments, which is equally important in making a hegemonic system acceptable to subaltern groups (Sassoon 2001). In yet another instantiation of determination in the first instance, material conditions do constrain the range of ideas and ideologies which can be successful in any given context. At the same time, there are at least two forms of relative autonomy that ideas and ideologies enjoy. On the one hand, these often outline significant changes in the material conditions that allowed for their rise in the first place. On the other hand, ideologies are also a device through which we decode reality and frame it in order to make sense of it, and successful ideologies end up influencing the way we perceive material factors, and by this they influence what we do about it and ultimately their transformation.

Articulation takes place not only within each of these dimensions, but also across them. The increased interconnection of the global economy, with the resulting 'time-space compression' (Harvey 1989), produced a change in the scalar dimension with significant consequences for material and ideational factors that is worth outlining by way of illustration. The existence of ever more integrated national economies means an intensification of relations between ruling groups from different states. Following from this, the material exchanges integral to the third

DOI: 10.1057/9781137395924

dimension on which hegemony is articulated take place not only within the national scale, but also across scales. A common case is the decision on the part of the ruling groups in peripheral countries to open up their economy to facilitate foreign investment, with the prospect of benefiting from the expected economic growth and by this consolidating their stability. In ideational terms, interscalar exchange is usually translated in the reliance on a 'conception of the world', as Gramsci used to put it, which has already become 'common sense' among the major players on the international scale. As discussed in the following chapters, both of these processes were clearly observable in Egypt.

This triple articulation allows us to substantially rework the meaning of hegemony beyond the one typical of existing neo-Gramscian approaches. Not dissimilarly from the Coxian perspective, hegemony is defined as a combination of coercion and consent, which 'balance each other reciprocally, without force predominating excessively over consent' (Gramsci 1971: 80, fn. 49). The strong subjective element carried by the adverb 'excessively' can be seen as an invitation to explore the different forms that hegemony takes, being from time to time more or less inclusive, more or less ideologically compelling, and ultimately more or less successful. Elaborating on Femia's typology (1981: 46–50), it is also possible to observe the evolution of hegemony over time as oscillating between the extremes of *integral* and *failed* hegemony. We are closer to the former when the overall society exhibits a substantial degree of 'moral and intellectual unity', and thus the ruling bloc obtains an almost unqualified commitment on the part of subaltern groups. Failed hegemony, on the other hand, sees the dissolution of this political and ideological bond cutting across social forces, leading either to raw coercion taking centre-stage to ensure the survival of the political order or directly to political disintegration.

However, hegemony as a balanced combination of coercion and consent does not take place in vacuum. And here the method of articulation proves extremely helpful in addressing the shortcomings of existing neo-Gramscian approaches. With respect to interscalar relations, the method of articulation allows us to overcome the understanding of the state as a 'transmission belt' of externally constructed hegemonies (Cox 1987; Robinson 2003 and 2004), showing instead how actors on the national scale are involved in the adaptation, domestication and potentially also subversion of external pressures. Applied to the interaction of economic and political factors, the method of articulation provides an antidote to both the state-centrism of accounts inspired by Cox and the class-centrism of the Amsterdam School (Worth 2008). Indeed, determination in the first instance and relative autonomy prevent a slide into economic determinism, but also permits to avoid multi-causality. As Gramsci put it, 'for though hegemony is ethico–political, it must also be economic, must necessarily be based on the decisive function exercised by the leading group in the decisive nucleus of economic activity' (1971: 161). Lastly, on the material–ideational dimension, arguing for the relevance of the material constitution of ideology allows us to understand how hegemonic projects are constructed and maintained not only by virtue of their ideological appeal, but are in the first instance determined by existing material conditions. At the same time, ideas can become a force of their own, influencing those material conditions that shaped their emergence in the first place.

Gramsci in Cairo: looking for hegemony in authoritarian contexts

The debate on how the relation between structure and superstructure should be conceptualised is at the heart of much debate in critical IPE. Neo-Gramscian accounts have been criticised from a Marxist standpoint for their 'pluralist empiricism', with the state and the market being treated as separate, and indeed opposed, forms of social organisation (Burnham 1991 and 1994). While potentially useful in analytical terms, the separation between capital and state as embodiments respectively of structure and superstructure is better treated as apparent, and as promoted by capitalist relations of production. In this respect, it is not inappropriate to conceptualise the relation between capital and state as emergent, as done by critical realist scholars (Jessop 2010; Joseph 2010), thus conceiving them as intimately related yet irreducible to each other.

Following Jessop (1990 and 2010), both capital and the state are better understood as social relations, and more specifically as *form-determined social relations*. This move is perfectly consistent with Gramsci's insistence on looking at the state 'in its inclusive sense', not merely in terms of state apparatus, but rather as 'an institutional ensemble' (1975: 1358–1361). State power then becomes 'a form-determined condensation of the changing balance of forces in political and politically relevant struggles' (Jessop 2010: 192). Similarly, if capital is conceived inclusively,

DOI: 10.1057/9781137395924

then 'capital accumulation is the complex resultant of the changing balance of class forces in struggle as they interact within a framework determined by the value form' (Jessop 1990: 197), intended as the fundamental relation linking together different elements – from production to circulation to distribution – and defining the parameters of capitalist development. In line with this tradition, the regulation school proposes the concept of *accumulation regime*, defined as 'the institutional ensemble and complex of norms which can secure capitalist reproduction *pro tempore* despite the antagonistic character of capitalist social relations' (Jessop 1990: 308).

In this study the discussion focuses on the change of accumulation regime in Egypt from *étatism* towards neoliberalism. The former is defined as an accumulation regime characterised by the predominant role of the state in the economy. More specifically, state intervention encompasses all the main aspects of economic activity: incentive-setting, planning, coordination, production, management and distribution (Wahba 1994; Ayubi 1995). *Étatism* also relies on the state for the management of 'the antagonist character of capitalist social relations' mentioned above, usually through a corporatist and/or populist arrangement aimed at containing social conflicts (Hinnebusch 1985; Ayubi 1995). On the other hand, *neoliberalism* is used here to identify an accumulation regime characterised by minimal direct intervention of the state in the economy, limited to setting up the legal, political and military functions required to guarantee the proper functioning of markets and their creation in those sectors where markets do not exist. Neoliberalisation – that is: the way by which a neoliberal accumulation regime is established – is characterised by four processes: privatisation of public assets, financialisation of the economy, management and manipulation of crises, state redistribution in favour of the upper classes (Harvey 2005: 159–165).[8]

The success of any given accumulation regime is related to the way in which political power is organised, and thus the specific form taken by the state. The form on which the literature insists the most is the *political regime*, intended here as a combination of procedural rules, formal or informal, determining in which way which actors can access which decision-making positions regulated by which rules, and the acceptance, strategic or normative, of this system by all the major actors involved (Munck 1996: 5–11). With respect to authoritarianism, the definition by Linz is still unsurpassed, and describes *authoritarian regimes* as

DOI: 10.1057/9781137395924

> political systems with limited, not responsible, pluralism, without elaborate or guiding ideologies, but with distinctive mentalities, without extensive or intensive political mobilisation, except at some points in their development, and in which a leader or occasionally a small group exercises power within formally ill-defined limits, but actually quite predictable ones. (1964: 255)

While this definition was obtained by contrasting the features of democracy and totalitarianism, the virtual disappearance of the latter does not make the definition any less valuable.

One should not forget that both capital accumulation and state power are social relations, and thus it is imperative to look at the specific social groups and how they are represented in the political regime, and at the balance of class forces and how they are embedded in the accumulation regime. With respect to the state, it is important to keep in mind that it has its own strategic selectivities, as Jessop put it (1990 and 2008). In other words, the state is not neutral in two fundamental ways. Firstly, and similarly to *path-dependency* approaches, past decisions always have an impact on current decisions, and this creates pressures bearing upon the courses of action that might be pursued by different actors. Secondly, the state also has a significant *path-shaping* power over actors, differentially empowering and disempowering specific actors, and thus creating an unevenly distributed configuration of constraints and opportunities. This is particularly visible in authoritarian contexts, with a variously defined elite enjoying considerable room to manoeuvre in the face of nearly powerless masses.

Within this context, Gramsci's concept of *ruling bloc* identifies a coalition of social groups constituting the base of support of a given political regime. Depending on its ability to win the consent of the majority of the population, a ruling bloc can also be a hegemonic bloc. The hegemony of the ruling bloc is then the precondition for the emergence of the conjunction of structure and superstructure at the heart of the historical bloc discussed earlier. Indeed, these links provide the material for one of the key questions addressed in this study, and namely, was the ruling bloc in Egypt under Mubarak also a hegemonic bloc?

On several occasions the reader will notice that the term *elites* is used interchangeably with the more precise ruling bloc. Elites are to be intended broadly as the social forces that 'wield political influence and power in that they make strategic decisions or participate in decision-making on a national level, contribute to define political norms and values (including the definition of "national interest"), and directly

DOI: 10.1057/9781137395924

influence political discourse on strategic issues' (Perthes 2004: 5). Is this focus on elites incompatible with a Gramscian approach? The *Prison Notebooks* contain several passages against elite theorists such as Mosca, Pareto and Michels. Yet, Gramsci's critique is a qualified one, as it suggests not the uselessness of the concept, but rather its neglect of 'relations of force', which belies the political objective of elite theory; discrediting the Marxist concept of the ruling class and replacing it with concepts such as 'political class' and 'the iron law of oligarchy', which obfuscate the class dimension implicit in political rule (1971: 6n, 150, 176).

It is thus imperative to look at social groups and their position in relations of production. Within the IPE literature, one way to move beyond the traditional distinction between rentier, bourgeois and working class is to follow Van der Pijl's work on class fractions distinguishing capital on the basis of its position in the accumulation circuit. We thus have productive capital, commodity capital (commercial), money capital (banking and financial) (Van der Pijl 1984: 3). This allows the researcher to expose potential fault lines within the same class. However, in contexts such as the Egyptian one where capital is highly fungible, and thus few business conglomerates stretch themselves between production, trade and finance, this distinction might be extremely difficult to pin down. Rather, given the pervasive presence of the state, it is worthwhile to begin from a threefold distinction of the groups constituting the Egyptian ruling bloc at the end of the 1980s. The first group, both in terms of size and power, was the public sector, and within it one could further differentiate between the army in a privileged position and the bureaucracy, including both managers of state-owned enterprises and highly ranked civil servants. The second component was the state-dependent *infitah* bourgeoisie, and the third was the landed elite temporarily sidelined under Nasser but gradually brought back into the fold of the regime by Sadat and Mubarak. Despite their disparate positions and internal differentiations, these groups – and the coalition they created – constituted the linchpin for the preservation of the authoritarian regime when Egypt was faced by fiscal crisis in the late 1980s. The industrial working class, the peasantry, the informal labour force, but also important sections of the middle classes, including small and medium entrepreneurs and self-employed professionals, were instead left behind by the gradual unravelling of the corporatist social pact.

As suggested in the introduction, the economic reforms of the 1990s and 2000s contributed significantly to the emergence of a new business

DOI: 10.1057/9781137395924

class. This could combine its links with key personalities in the regime with much stronger relations with transnational capital than the *infitah* bourgeoisie. While this new group was supposed to revitalise and restructure authoritarian rule under a more profitable and thus sustainable accumulation regime, it failed to provide a new lasting basis for a reformed authoritarian regime. Instead of steering an evolution in this direction, economic reforms appear to have contributed in no minor way to the emergence and deepening of a fracture between the different components of the regime, effectively providing strong reasons for discontent in that very section of the ruling bloc – the army – which was also the last backstop against social unrest.[9]

While within-regime changes are crucial to understand the weakening of the regime, to grasp the full magnitude of the social transformations produced by these reforms it is imperative to locate these power shifts in broader social relations. The outcome of the struggle between the new business class and the army had substantial implications for the direction and pace of the reforms implemented. This in turn had a broader effect on the distribution of wealth and resources in the whole country. Thus, an appreciation of the impact of economic reforms also on the various sections of the middle class, as well as the lower social classes, particularly peasants, industrial workers and the informal proletariat, should allow us to avoid falling into the trap of writing what Morton calls a 'political economy of lordships' (2007: 49).

Once transformations within the ruling bloc are located within broader social relations and are combined with the analysis of effects also on groups outside of the regime circuit, the study of economic reforms implemented in the 1990s and 2000s should take us a step closer to understanding the deeper socio-economic causes of the Egyptian revolution.

Conclusion

The dynamics of the Egyptian revolution are captured partially at best by mainstream approaches dealing with the relation between economic and political transformations in authoritarian regimes. Mass participation and protests, which started in Egypt on 25 January 2011, and which has had very recently another iteration leading to Morsi's overthrow, would already suggest that there was something that both modernisation theory

DOI: 10.1057/9781137395924

and the predatory elite thesis were unable to account for. The former would in fact expect the path towards democracy to take the form of a negotiated transition that would involve the incumbent elites and the leaders of the emerging middle class. The outpouring of protesters in Tahrir Square and beyond, and thus the genuine mass dimension of the Egyptian revolution seems to point towards a process that went well beyond relatively small sections of society. The predatory elite thesis, on other hand, would expect no transition at all, or at least a controlled process of opening, what Hinnebusch called 'calculated decompression' (1985). Now, whereas it is true that the latest events appear to point towards a return of the *ancien régime*, it is undeniable that things have already changed way beyond the point of no return, in that now Egypt is experiencing a wave of sustained mobilisation that is not likely to peter out any time soon. To be successful, the current attempt at reinstating the same alliance characterising the Mubarak regime would require systematic resort to coercion in order to repress not only the Muslim Brotherhood, but also the secular and leftist demonstrators who are strongly opposed to a return to the army-dominated past.

This reference to a greater reliance on coercion than consent on the part of the army also suggests that an explanation rooted in Gramsci's work has much to offer to the analysis of the Egyptian case. More specifically, this chapter has argued that a Gramscian approach able to recover the philosophy of praxis, and the concept of articulation stemming thereof, is extremely well suited to grasp the magnitude and direction of the political and ideological transformations experienced by developing countries which have been trying to reform their economy following the neoliberal template supported by IFIs, main donors and investors. In this respect, the focus on articulation serves not the scope of developing an alternative Gramscian *theory*, but rather to suggest how Gramsci can provide the foundations of an alternative *method* for studying continuities and transformations in the global political economy. As a consequence of being a method, there is no specific prediction leading from cause A to effect B, but rather an open-ended matrix to be investigated on a case-by-case basis.

At the same time, if articulation is intended as determination in the first instance on the one hand and relative autonomy on the other hand, it is possible to develop an account which traces back changes in relations of force within the regime to the position within society of the empowered and/or weakened factions, while also investigating the impact on social

DOI: 10.1057/9781137395924

groups excluded from the ruling bloc. I contend that such an approach is able to account in a more complete and more nuanced way than existing ones for the preconditions underpinning the increasing social tensions that resulted in the 2011 Egyptian revolution. Discussing and corroborating this claim is the task I shall undertake in the following chapters.

Notes

1   A clarification is in order here. In this study, democratisation theory is defined as the grand theory, largely developed in the footsteps of Lipset's seminal study (1959), identifying a correlation between a range of factors including – but not limited to – economic development and the emergence of democratic political systems. While certainly related, democratisation theory and the literature on democratic transitions are different bodies of work and thought, and the latter – better exemplified by the fine-grained accounts included in O'Donnell, Schmitter and Whitehead (1986) – is excluded from the scope of this book.

2   On the conflict between political and economic logic, see Heydemann (1992) and Schlumberger (2008). On state restructuring and repositioning in order to adapt to economic pressures, see Owen (2001) and Tripp (2001).

3   See respectively Nelson (1989) and Haggard and Kaufman (1992) on distributional coalitions, and Heydemann (2004) on informal networks.

4   On the former see for example Rupert (1995). On the latter, good examples are provided by Van der Pjil (1998) and Van Apeldoorn (2002).

5   See respectively, Cox (1981, 1983 and 1987) and Van der Pijl (1984 and 1998). For attempts at dealing with developing countries, see Moore (2007) on South Korea, Gray (2010) on China, Shields (2012) on Poland.

6   The first explicit formulation of this phrase to characterise Gramsci's thought is found in Luporini (1958: 42).

7   Nazih Ayubi constitutes once more an exception in this respect, as articulation is crucial in his study of the political economy of the Middle East (1995).

8   While inspired by Harvey, the decision of linking these four processes directly to neoliberalism is also a move away from his work, where instead these processes are equated with 'accumulation by dispossession'. The latter should in my view have a more circumscribed role and refer to the persistence of forms of primitive accumulation that draw new resources within the circuit of capital. Some of the processes mentioned above, instead, are better seen as redistribution of resources already inserted in the circuit of capital accumulation. I would like to thank Alex Callinicos for bringing this point to my attention.

DOI: 10.1057/9781137395924

9   Despite its relative weakening *vis-à-vis* the new business class, one should
    not forget that the army retains a measure of autonomy from the regime as
    it controls a parallel economy constituted of 'military industries engaged in
    non-military production', as Hanna Kheir-el-Din put it during one of our
    conversations (Cairo, 4 May 2010). Unfortunately, the analysis of the military
    economy is precluded to most analysts, with two interesting exceptions being
    a chapter in Springborg's seminal book on the political economy of the first
    decade of Mubarak's rule (1989) and the recent short piece by Marshall and
    Stacher (2012).

DOI: 10.1057/9781137395924

2
The Egyptian Way to Neoliberalism? IMF, World Bank and Reforms in Egypt

Abstract: *Through the analysis of the interaction between national and international institutions, this chapter reconstructs the international political economy of reforms in Egypt under Mubarak. While it provides room for showing how reforms were delayed, diluted and at times opposed, the method of articulation allows us to see that two decades of reforms had decidedly transformed the Egyptian economy in a neoliberal direction.*

Keywords: institutions; neoliberalism; Egyptianisation; economic reforms

Roccu, Roberto. *The Political Economy of the Egyptian Revolution: Mubarak, Economic Reforms and Failed Hegemony*. Basingstoke: Palgrave Macmillan, 2014. DOI: 10.1057/9781137395924.

DOI: 10.1057/9781137395924

Relations between international financial institutions and the Egyptian government have usually been analysed in two ways. On the one hand, there is a sizeable area studies literature suggesting that the pressures towards reforms on the part of the IMF and the World Bank, but also main donors and investors, have not been strong enough to force the Mubarak regime out of a long-established path of patrimonial capitalism (Schlumberger 2008). While the government has not been opposed altogether to the demands on IFIs, it is argued, it has engaged in 'the politics of dilatory reform' (Richards 1991). On the other hand, there is a relatively smaller literature which has instead maintained that already before the sweeping reforms implemented under ERSAP, there had been a much increased penetration of foreign capital and more generally globalising forces within the Egyptian economy (Zaalouk 1989). Whereas neither of these traditions is entirely off track, and indeed accounts for a significant part of the story, closer empirical scrutiny suggests that something more nuanced is needed in order to grasp both the substantial transformation experienced by the Egyptian economy since the 1990s and the significant role still played by national actors despite Egypt's increased integration in the global political economy.

The focus on interscalar articulation of this chapter should put us in the position of assessing elements of both continuity and change in the Egyptian political economy. Contrary to what will be discussed in the following chapters, the analytical focus here is not as much on social classes as on institutions, both on the national and the international scale. This choice is motivated by two reasons. Firstly, on a more theoretical level, an indirect link with the Gramscian insights can be maintained if institutions are considered as forms of condensation of social relations from which specific drives towards accumulation regimes and hegemonic projects may stem. Secondly, when reforms started foreign private capital played a relatively minor role compared to other countries at comparable levels of development. It is then not unreasonable to assume that the first steps towards a thorough transformation of the Egyptian economy must come from somewhere else, and more specifically from institutional dynamics. Furthermore, in order to change an *étatist* accumulation regime, one needs to engage first and foremost with the dominant actors within the existing system, and thus the state itself, its institutions and the ruling bloc controlling them. This is the reason why this chapter focuses mostly on the interaction between the Egyptian government and IFIs. This is done more specifically through the use of process-tracing in order to

DOI: 10.1057/9781137395924

detect whether the timing, sequencing and most importantly content of reforms implemented corresponded, and to which degree, to the reforms promoted by IFIs and usually understood under the label of 'Washington Consensus'. Thus, the letter of the agreements with IMF and World Bank has been contrasted against the main reform bills passed by the Egyptian parliament, from agriculture to manufacturing to finance.[1]

In this way, the method of articulation allows us to develop a layered account of the international political economy of reforms. The first layer effectively shows that the socio-economic impact of reforms implemented amounted to a neoliberalisation of the Egyptian economy. The first two sections help us reach this conclusion by respectively discussing how IFIs approached the Egyptian government in the wake of the late 1980s fiscal crisis and what were the results of the reforms implemented, both negotiated with international institutions and autonomously carried out by the government. The second layer instead allows us to understand that both reforms and outcomes contained distinctly Egyptian elements. This is discussed with reference to several instances of delay, dilution, but also subversion and transformation of reforms. Importantly, and here is where social relations come back, the government's ability to insert unorthodox elements in their reforms increased as the outward-oriented faction of private capital became more important within the ruling bloc.

The globalisers facing structural crisis: Egypt and the Washington Consensus

By the end of the 1980s, the Egyptian political economy was characterised by three key elements. Firstly, during the whole period between the Free Officers' coup and 1990 the Egyptian economy was a structurally dependent one. While the forms of dependency might have changed over time, its essence was not altered by Nasser's nationalisations nor by Sadat's economic opening. Indeed, matters in this respect worsened under *infitah*, as the decision to scale back the developmental function while keeping the welfarist one had severely damaging consequences for the state. The decrease in revenues was combined with the maintenance of social programmes, crucial to regime legitimation, leading to the build up of an unmanageable stock of debt (Ikram 2006). Secondly, ever since the sequestrations and nationalisations in the wake of the

DOI: 10.1057/9781137395924

Suez canal crisis, activities in the Egyptian economy had largely been controlled by locals, be they army officials, public sector managers or members of the *infitah* bourgeoisie (Wahba 1994). This aspect is of particular relevance because it sets Egypt apart from most other peripheral countries, characterised as they were by the domination of foreign capital (Cardoso 1979). Lastly, despite the *infitah*, it would be unreasonable to think of the Egyptian economy as a liberalised one. At best we could talk of a shift *within* the *étatist* paradigm, with the state surrendering only a part of its functions related to production and management, but keeping its dominant role with respect to incentive-setting, planning, coordination and distribution. By 1990, the total capital of private companies amounted to less than 10 per cent of book value of the state sector (Ayubi 1995: 349).

Thus, the dominant position of the state in the Egyptian economy in the late 1980s can hardly be overstated. In much the same way, the troubles in which the economy was in that specific conjuncture can hardly be overestimated too. By the mid-1980s, the chronic indebtedness was worsened by a sharp drop in oil prices, forcing the Egyptian government to enter in negotiations with the IMF and sign a stabilisation package worth SDR250 million (Abdel-Khalek 2001: 25). While the commitment on the part of the government faltered as soon as the situation appeared to improve, this was the first step towards an ever greater involvement of IFIs in the national economy, which arguably found its peak in the Economic Reform and Structural Adjustment Programme signed with both the IMF and the World Bank respectively in May and November 1991.

These reforms were theoretically grounded in the neoclassical synthesis, which on the one hand rejected the fiscal activism typical of the 1950s and 1960s and on the other hand required the government to be even more activist in its monetary policy. However, monetary policy was not to be modelled anymore around the trade-off between unemployment and inflation as conceptualised in the Phillips curve, but rather should be focusing on maintaining price stability. Even more importantly, the new policy paradigm was based on a widespread belief in the ineffectiveness of barriers to capital movements (Chwieroth 2010). Starting from these theoretical tenets, it only made sense for IFIs to suggest developing countries to abandon the *étatist* or classical developmentalist path and follow the policy directions suggested in Table 2.1. For the sake of analytical conciseness, the principles of the Washington Consensus

DOI: 10.1057/9781137395924

TABLE 2.1   *Washington consensus*

1.	Fiscal discipline
2.	Redirection of public expenditure away from generalised subsidies and towards education and health
3.	Tax reform (lower marginal tax rate and broadened tax base)
4.	Interest rates liberalisation
5.	Competitive exchange rates
6.	Trade liberalisation
7.	Liberalisation of inflow of FDI
8.	Privatisation
9.	Deregulation
10.	Secure property rights

Source: Williamson 1989.

could be further summarised into three groups. Firstly, general macroeconomic policies aiming at combining fiscal balance or surplus with sustained growth. An important corollary of this element is the relatively narrow understanding of what macroeconomic policy should be, which translates into an attempt at reducing drastically the presence of the state in the economy, for example through the privatisation of public sector enterprises. Secondly, the liberalisation of the financial sector with respect to both capital movements and banking sector ownership. Thirdly, trade liberalisation in both its internal (abolition of price controls and phasing out of subsidies) and external (progressive reduction of tariff and non-tariff barriers) components.

If this was the reform plan supported by IFIs, and Egypt's main creditors, in a moment in which the national economy badly needed external assistance, how could these reforms alter the face of the Egyptian economy? According to both liberals and surprisingly many critical IPE scholars, not infrequently also neo-Gramscian ones, the international scale is likely to transform altogether the national economy.[2] This is relatively straightforward for liberals, as trade and capital flows will expose developing countries to worldwide competition, and thus force domestic companies, both public and private, to become more efficient in order not to lose their market shares in the national economy and possibly also gain market shares abroad. Even though phrased in an entirely different language, the conclusion of much critical IPE literature points in the same direction. More specifically, the argument here is that the spread of neoliberal globalisation, effected by agents

DOI: 10.1057/9781137395924

including but not limited to IFIs, has led to the increased dominance of global and transnational factors over national ones. Already in his 1981 article Cox suggested that the internationalisation of production had led to the emergence of a 'transnational managerial class' (1981: 147). Stephen Gill went further in arguing that the transnationalisation of production had led within both capital and labour to alliances cutting across national boundaries both for and against this process (1995). The combination of these elements leads in their view to a weakening of the state, which could take place in two different ways. Firstly, through the rise of actors beyond the reach of state power, such as multinational corporations, informal directorates such as the Trilateral Commission and the Bildenberg group (Gill 1990), and last but not least the IMF and the World Bank (Murphy 1994). Secondly, the same outcome of state weakening could also materialise through the increasing penetration of social forces promoting transnationalisation into the state apparatus (Cox 1992: 31). Is this what actually happened in the Egyptian case? A look at the reform process over the past two decades might help us in understanding whether this is the case.

Going neoliberal? The transformation of the Egyptian economy

Reforms in Egypt did not take place smoothly and uncontroversially as it might have happened in other developing countries that engaged with the IFIs since the 1980s. This is due both to the *étatist* and nationalist tradition characterising the Egyptian political economy and economic policy-making and to its bargaining power, comparatively larger than that of most other developing countries because of its strategic impor- tance in an oil-rich region such as the Middle East. For this reason, reforms in Egypt were patchy and somehow inconsistent, with phases of thorough compliance alternating with periods of stasis and outright backlash. However, if one is to look at the three broad dimensions of reform touched upon by the Washington Consensus, then it is undeni- able that Egypt fared remarkably well, to the point of being repeatedly praised by both the IMF and the World Bank.

On the macroeconomic dimension, the stabilisation measures con- tained in ERSAP followed very closely the first five objectives listed in Table 2.1. More specifically, fiscal discipline, and particularly budget deficit reduction, was at the very core of the stabilisation package. To meet the stringent fiscal targets, the government was required to cut significantly public expenditure, something it had always been reluctant to do since the 1977 riots associated with the withdrawal of bread subsidies. Even though a comprehensive tax reform proved unfeasible, incremental changes in the tax system provided a broadening of the tax base and the imposition of a General Sales Tax (Soliman 2011: 109–13). This was compounded by several changes in monetary policy, with the removal of credit ceilings, the full-fledged liberalisation of interest rates and the unification of the exchange rate for the Egyptian pound (LE) at the level of the most devalued rate.

Considered along the IMF guidelines, the stabilisation programme was remarkably successful (IMF 1997: 4). Inflation fell from an average of 19 per cent a year during the 1987–91 period to 4.6 per cent in 1997. The budget deficit was drastically reduced, from 15.3 per cent in 1991 to 1.3 per cent in 1996, 'an effort that has perhaps few international parallels in history' (ibid: 7). As a result of changes in monetary policy, the level of dollarisation of the economy and the annual rate of liquidity growth also fell considerably under the stabilisation programme. The unification of the exchange rate led to an increase in revenues, particularly from oil and Suez canal receipts, which combined with a reduction of budgetary expenditure by 7.5 per cent and cancellation of half of the debt on the part of Paris Club countries was fundamental to deficit reduction (Ikram 2006: 67).

As mentioned above, even though not directly included in macroeconomic stabilisation, privatisation also had to do with the decision to demand a less interventionist role of the state in the economy. Even though not as wide-ranging as demanded by IFIs, privatisation during the second half of the 1990s led to the sale of more than a hundred state-owned enterprises, with a total sales value of more than LE14 billion. In 1998, the Egyptian programme was ranked fourth in the world in terms of privatisation receipts as a share of GDP (IMF 1998: 52). Not long after these rankings were published, *The Economist* ran a story on the virtuous relation finally developing between IFIs and the national government, defining Egypt 'the IMF's model pupil' (18 March 1999). After a major slowdown in economic activity related to the East Asian crisis, and a corresponding halt to privatisations, a new wave starting in 2004 broke the prolonged sluggishness. Under the newly launched Asset Management Programme, the Ministry of Investment oversaw the sale of 130 state-owned assets between 2004 and 2007, with proceeds in

DOI: 10.1057/9781137395924

excess of LE46 billion.[3] During this second phase, privatisations went as far as touching previously off-limits sector, including cement, oil refineries and banks.

The sale of state-owned shares in joint-venture banks was indeed one of the two dimensions of financial sector reform. While these measures encountered remarkable opposition within the ruling circles for more than a decade, there was a remarkable turn of the tide when a new cabinet headed by the 'reformist' Ahmed Nazif was appointed in 2004. By the end of 2006, 94 per cent of state-owned shares in joint-venture banks had been divested (World Bank 2006: 11, ft. 10), and 80 per cent of the smallest public-sector bank, Bank of Alexandria, was sold to Banca San Paolo (later Intesa San Paolo). As shown in Table 2.2, by June 2010 public banks accounted for 45 per cent of total assets and 44 per cent of total deposits, with private banks holding for the first time since 1960 the majority of both assets and deposits (World Bank 2010b: 58). Whereas these numbers are not terribly impressive if compared to the Eastern European countries touched by 'shock therapy' reforms in the 1990s, they do in fact signal a sea change in the specific Egyptian case.

Capital account liberalisation, together with Law 95 of 1992, contributed to the effective relaunching of the stock exchange (ARE 1992a), which until that point had fallen 'into a deep sleep' (Roll 2010: 352). While the original aim was to make it the prime intermediary for privatisations

TABLE 2.2   *Ownership structure of the banking sector (1990–2010)*[4]

	1990	1992	1994	1996	1998	2000	2002	2004	2008	2010
Assets										
Public banks	56.8	63.9	63.7	61.6	59.3	58.6	58.6	60.4	47.4	45.4
Commercial	49.3	57.0	57.8	55.7	52.8	51.7	52.0	53.9	41.9	40.8
Specialised	7.5	6.9	5.9	5.9	6.5	6.9	6.6	6.5	5.5	4.6
Private banks	43.2	36.1	36.3	38.4	40.7	41.4	41.4	39.6	52.6	54.6
Joint venture	–	–	–	–	–	–	–	20.8	1.3	1.7
Private	–	–	–	–	–	–	–	18.8	51.3	52.9
Deposits										
Public banks	61.5	67.6	69.9	66.9	64.0	61.8	60.4	60.1	47.1	44.2
Commercial	59.0	65.7	67.5	63.1	60.1	57.3	56.1	54.5	41.9	40.2
Specialised	2.5	1.9	2.4	3.8	3.9	4.5	4.3	5.6	5.2	4.0
Private banks	38.5	32.4	30.1	33.1	36.0	38.2	39.6	39.9	52.9	55.8
Joint venture	–	–	–	–	-	-	-	20.7	1.1	1.4
Private	–	–	–	–	-	-	-	19.2	51.8	54.4

Source: CBE archives; estimates for 2010 from World Bank 2010b.

DOI: 10.1057/9781137395924

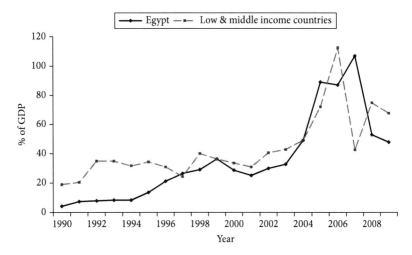

FIGURE 2.1   *Market capitalisation of listed companies as share of GDP (1990–2009)*
Source: World Bank 2010a.

(Shams El-Din 1998: 147), during the 2000s it managed to reach the same levels of capitalisation of countries at comparable levels of development (see Figure 2.1). However, this does not mean that capital markets managed at any point to threaten the dominance of the financial sector on the part of banks.

With respect to trade liberalisation, the removal of external barriers, starting from tariffs, had already begun before the signing of ERSAP and continued at faster pace afterwards. Import bans were for example reduced from 210 items in 1991 to 26 in 1993, export bans from 20 to 2, and products subject to quantitative export quotas from 17 to 4. On the internal side of liberalisation, price controls were gradually phased out, and so were most subsidies, with the items still covered by them falling from 18 in the late 1970s to 4 in 2000. Unsurprisingly, these transformations also had significant side effects, visible for example in the significant increase in foreign direct investment inflows witnessed by Figure 2.2.

In sum, while not entirely satisfactory, on the parameters of interest to IFIs economic reforms went a long way in transforming the national economy in the direction hoped for by international organisations, main donors and investors. This was also reflected in generally positive, if somewhat inconsistent, growth trends, and in increasing trade and capital flows with the EU on the regional level.[5] Thus, the success narrative

DOI: 10.1057/9781137395924

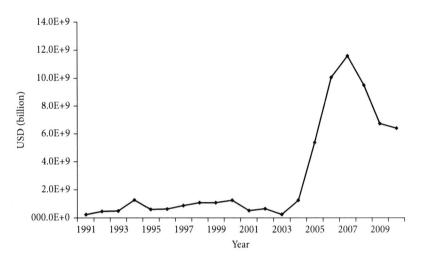

FIGURE 2.2   *FDI net inflows (1991–2010)*
Sources: World Bank (2010a).

employed by both IFIs and local policy-makers did have some empirical elements to cling on to.

Beyond the mere aggregate level, these reforms also had significant consequences with respect to power relations. In this respect it is helpful to look at what has happened in agriculture and manufacturing, which constituted the heart of the populist social contract, and in the financial sector, which is admittedly one of the main channels by which neoliberalism penetrated and was consolidated in several developing countries. In agriculture, the new tenancy law – Law 96 of 1992 – liberalised rents after a five-year transition period, gave owners the possibility to buy back the contract from the tenant, whereas until then the tenancy contract was in principle valid in perpetuity, and also the right to evict the tenant if the land was to be sold and there was no agreement between the two (ARE 1992b). In order to settle owner–tenant conflicts, a reconciliation committee was established, but its impartiality was questioned from several quarters (Bush 1999: 46; Saad 2002: 120). According to Mitchell (2002: 265), the full implementation of the law in 1997 saw the eviction of almost a million peasants and the loss of more than 700,000 jobs. Looking back at the definition of neoliberalisation adopted in this study, this might well be considered a case of management and manipulation of crisis in favour of a specific social group – the landlords – and at the same time of state redistribution of resources on highly regressive terms.

DOI: 10.1057/9781137395924

Following from this, there has been a dramatic increase in rural inequality (Fergany 2002: 219–29). By the turn of the century landholding had become more unequal than before 1952, with 2,281 holders (0.05 per cent of total) accounting for 11 per cent of total landholding area. Widespread violence in the countryside was another consequence of these reforms (MALR 2000). According to Land Center for Human Rights (LCHR), an NGO providing legal advice to farmers and raising awareness of deteriorating living conditions in rural Egypt, more than 800 tenants were killed in land disputes following the full implementation of the new law, and more than 7,000 were arrested.[6]

In manufacturing, privatisations allowed by Law 203 of 1991 (ARE 1991), trade and price liberalisation and the removal of energy subsidies had a major impact both on output and on income distribution in the sector. On the former, a rather persuasive case has been made suggesting that because of such reforms Egypt suffered from de-industrialisation (Abdel-Khalek 2001). Other than to rising costs, this also related to the way privatisations were conducted, with public monopolies often being replaced by private ones. Following from this, newly privatised companies had little incentive to become competitive abroad as long as they were able to dominate the local market. With respect to income distribution, the preservation of the ten-year tax exemption for new manufacturing activities in the new industrial cities created for this purpose were combined with a marginal cut in both corporate and industrial tax (Soliman 2011: 123–4). Whereas there is not enough disaggregate data on this aspect, it is safe to assume that these measures increased the available income for entrepreneurs investing in the tax-free zones, whereas income taxes weighed on industrial workers as much as they did in the past, being now combined with the General Sales Tax. This worsening in the relative conditions of the industrial working class was further exacerbated by the major lay-offs which took place in newly privatised companies. It should not come as a surprise that the reaction to this was a surge in labour activism (Beinin and El-Hamalawy 2007a and 2007b), considered by the foremost expert on the Egyptian working classes as 'the largest and most sustained social movement in Egypt since the campaign to oust the British occupiers after World War II' (Beinin 2007).

In the financial sector, the measures adopted under the auspices of ERSAP, ranging from a speculative mini-boom through the hike in interest rates to the issuing of tax-free treasury bonds, amounted to a fiscal subsidy for banks that by 1996/97 was estimated to be worth

DOI: 10.1057/9781137395924

about 10 per cent of GDP (IMF 1997: 35). Thus, the costs of the crisis were borne by those large swathes of society with limited or no access to financial instruments, with banks reaping handsome benefits in a textbook case of redistribution of resources away from the average citizen towards those in the 'commanding heights' of the domestic financial sector.

Thus, if neoliberalisation is to be intended as a combination of privatisation, financialisation, management and manipulation of crisis, and state redistribution in favour of the upper classes, then Egypt had certainly made significant strides in this direction since the late 1980s. However, this shift towards a neoliberal accumulation regime need not imply that the state had surrendered to the demands of global capital accumulation and ever-greater penetration of international capital. In this respect, there is another strand of literature that takes as its starting point exactly the overpowering position of the state within the Egyptian political economy at the end of 1980s. In the extremely clear exposition by Schlumberger (2008), this argument proceeds as follows. Over time, the Middle East has consolidated itself as a region characterised by a concentrated political control over the economy, and thus typically by authoritarian systems of rule and by the prevalence of informal modes of interaction, such as patronage and *wasta*, over formal ones. This provides for a heavily hierarchical political system, which puts the state, and thus the regime and the supporting coalition, in an ideal position to defuse the pressures built by IFIs and other agents of neoliberal globalisation. Following from this privileged position on the national scale, the regime and its main components are largely in control of any reform process initiated, and thus have an incentive to implement only those measures that are unlikely to threaten – or likely to bolster – their position. Thus, in times of crisis and under the spectre of conditionality, some reforms are implemented because under severe economic pressure any form of assistance or debt relief is welcome. However, policies that are considered as having the potential of endangering the status quo, and thus the stranglehold of the incumbent regime on political power, are either opposed, or delayed indefinitely, or implemented selectively (ibid: 630). Following from this, the dominance of the state and the regime in the national political economy translates into a manipulation of economic processes for political purposes. Indeed, there were clearly attempts in this direction on the part of some sections of the ruling bloc, and these are the main subject of the following section.

DOI: 10.1057/9781137395924

Egyptianising neoliberalism? Articulations on the national scale

Whereas the general thrust of reforms appears to conform to the demands of IFIs, this does not necessarily mean that the process by which this happened was a smooth and uncontroversial one. Rather, empirical evidence suggests that reforms were much more contested than crude numbers would lead us to think. Indeed, it is exactly through instances of delay, dilution, partial implementation and on some occasions also backtracking and outright opposition that the Egyptian ruling bloc attempted to use its bargaining power in order to bend neoliberal reforms to its goals of maintaining and consolidating its own position within a reformed political economy. In other words, it is here that we should look at to understand whether the political logic of power maintenance took precedence over the logic of economic efficiency (Heydemann 1992).

The float of the Egyptian pound is an excellent case in point, as during the early 1990s the Egyptian government did not prove particularly receptive to the demands coming from the IMF and the World Bank (Momani 2005). Pound devaluation was at the top of the IMF wishlist, as the export-led model promoted through the Washington Consensus was based on a competitive exchange rate. However, at that stage the government considered this measure to be unsustainable, and probably with good reasons, as such a move would have increased substantially both the import bill and the dollarisation of the economy, and would have constituted a disincentive for Egyptian workers abroad to send their remittances home.[7] Thus, what was pursued in this phase was the lowest-common denominator outcome of the unification of the exchange rate at the level of the most devalued rate. The deadlock on devaluation proved so tough to break that by 1995 the IMF dropped this demand (EIU 1996: 18). Perhaps surprisingly, the issue of devaluation was autonomously tackled by the government in the early 2000s firstly abandoning the fixed exchange rate towards a managed peg and then announcing the floating of the pound in January 2003 (EIU 2003: 18–21). The devaluations during the managed peg and the first six months of floating amounted to a depreciation of about 40 per cent against the US dollar (OANDA 2011), leading to an uncharacteristic – given the lack of formal agreements in place – statement of support on the part of the IMF (2003).

DOI: 10.1057/9781137395924

Something very similar, although with a slightly different timing, happened also with respect to the privatisation of public and joint-venture banks, already touched upon earlier. In January 1993, under the World Bank's threat that the second tranche of its loan would be withdrawn, the government committed to estimate the value of joint-venture banks, with the prospect of divesting state-owned shares (IMF 1993a). This divestiture together with the privatisation of one public bank was among the conditions attached to the three-year Extended Fund Facility approved by the IMF (1993b: 313). Under the pressure of debt cancellation to be decided in mid-July 1994, the government partially complied with these demands, selling its shares in 11 joint-venture banks, but without touching the big four public banks (Momani 2005: 55). The privatisation of a public sector bank was also a condition of the 1996 Stand-by Arrangement, but the government did not comply with it, without suffering any consequences. As in the case of devaluation, policy change was largely endogenous, taking place following the new Central Banking law in late 2003 and the appointment of the Nazif cabinet in July 2004. As mentioned above, almost all of the state-owned shares in joint-venture banks had been divested by the end of 2006, Bank of Alexandria had effectively been privatised, and Bank Misr and Banque du Caire were merged with a view to privatisation that was postponed due to adverse market conditions in the wake of the global financial crisis (Mohieldin and Nasr 2007: 719).

These two instances suggest two considerations regarding the thesis suggested that neoliberalisation would lead to a dominance of transnational over national forces. On the one hand, the ability of the regime with respect to delaying reforms and autonomously deciding their timing and sequencing suggests that the state was never merely a 'transmission belt' as maintained by Cox and Robinson. On the other hand, it showed that in fact reforms proceeded more smoothly in the direction preferred by IFIs once they were carried out by national policy-makers without much interference from international organisations.[8] To some degree, this would seem to support the World Bank's view that reform 'ownership' on the part of national institutions helps. This was further witnessed by the remarks of minister of investment Mahmoud Mohieldin, who suggested that 'when you have your own agenda, you can always get people behind you'.[9]

Reforms in agriculture are instead extremely helpful for understanding the politics of backtracking and of selective implementation, and

DOI: 10.1057/9781137395924

give us the chance to investigate the nature of neoliberalisation in Egypt. Under the leadership of Yusuf Wali as minister of agriculture,[10] and with the strong support on the part of World Bank and USAID (World Bank 1993 and 2001), this sector was the pioneer of structural reforms.[11] For our purposes, it is useful to highlight the contrast with respect to the implementation of the reform on fertiliser provision and of the new tenancy law. On the former, until the 1980s both inputs and fertilisers were provided by the state-owned Principal Bank for Development and Agricultural Credit (PBDAC) at a subsidised price. The dismantlement of public sector monopoly in fertiliser provision led to the emergence of an oligopoly controlled by three companies. Their cartel practices led to a fourfold increase in local price between 1994 and 1996. However, the price of LE400 per tonne was still well below the export price of LE800, which thus led private companies to prefer exporting rather than selling in the domestic market. Unsurprisingly, an acute crisis of undersupply forced PBDAC to restart public sector provision of fertilisers already in 1995 (Bush 1999). On the other hand, there were very few second-thoughts concerning the implementation of the new tenancy law, despite the expected – and systematically realised – social costs involved. As noted, external agencies played a very minor role in the drafting and discussion of the law itself (Hinnebusch 1993: 21–2). In 1997, at the end of the transitional period, the government did not show much hesitation in allowing land takeover and the eviction of tenants.

These two cases tell us something very interesting regarding the lopsided character of neoliberalism in Egypt, which in turn led to an integration within the global economy which was 'differential' at best. More specifically, the willingness to proceed regardless of the social consequences with the implementation of the new tenure law shows a tendency on the part of the government to privilege dispossession over the alleged objectives of state withdrawal and a more competitive economy. The management of the crisis in fertiliser provision similarly suggests that whenever the state is needed for the market not to break down (as what was experienced was clearly a case of market failure), it is allowed to step in even though this means constraining competition. In other words, capital accumulation appears to be the main priority: in agriculture, trade liberalisation and land dispossession are more func-tional to this goal than the liberalisation of input provision, which can be sacrificed if 'social peace' – one of the linchpins of the political discourse under Mubarak – is perceived to be at stake.

DOI: 10.1057/9781137395924

The insertion of genuinely innovative elements, at times somewhat idiosyncratic with the standard neoliberal template, was a third way by which the regime attempted to control and 'domesticate' the most problematic aspects of reform. Two examples are particularly fitting in this regard. In 2005, the Ministry of Trade and Industry launched the National Supplier Development Programme (NSDP) with the aim of modernising the manufacturing sector also downstream, thus providing funding and technical assistance to SMEs supplying large companies in all sectors (EIU 2005: 30). Other than being an eminently interventionist way of diffusing reforms beyond large companies, the way in which the programme was devised cast serious doubts on the chances of actually achieving the proposed aim. More specifically, the government contacted large companies (37 before the launch of the programme, about one hundred during the whole process), which would then extend the project to their smaller suppliers. It is not difficult to see how such a plan might have served more the purpose of strengthening the ties between the regime and large companies rather than actually improving the efficiency of small and medium suppliers.

The second example comes from the Asset Management Programme, which had repeatedly won the praise of the World Bank in its yearly *Doing Business Report*, with Egypt being included among the top-ten reformers for four years out of five between 2005 and 2009.[12] In 2008, as the financial crisis reduced global liquidity and thus the potential for profitably divesting state-owned companies and social unrest was growing in newly privatised companies, Mohieldin proposed a shift away from privatisations towards public-private partnerships (PPPs) as the privileged form of state-asset management (EIU 2010: 6). Once again, this would point both to the increased autonomy of national policy-makers with respect to the content of policies and their willingness to use this room to manoeuvre for articulating economic reforms in a way that would not threaten regime stability.

At the end of the day, as Mohieldin aptly put it during our interview, 'Egypt is no country for shock therapy'.[13] Thus, delays, selective implementations and original articulations away from the neoliberal template were all strategies aimed at preventing the risk of a social collapse such as the one that Russia faced during the Yeltsin era. At the same time, slowly but steadily, the Egyptian economy was undergoing a process of thorough restructuring, within which national policy-makers were enjoying increasing autonomy as their reformist credentials came to be

DOI: 10.1057/9781137395924

accepted by IFIs. This increased trust became apparent once the most business-friendly and outward-oriented fraction became dominant within the ruling National Democratic Party (NDP). The use of this autonomy was always meant to be a risky business. On the one hand, it might have served the purpose of controlling the pace of reforms in order to preserve social stability. On the other hand, it could be used in the attempt of bolstering regime prospects, and possibly strengthening one component within the ruling bloc at the expense of the others but also of wider society. All of these aspects will be discussed in much greater depth in the next chapter.

Conclusion

Through the analysis of the interaction between national and international institutions, this chapter has identified three main trends characterising the influence of interscalar relations on the political economy of reforms in Egypt. In the first place, the international scale constituted an inescapable constraint on the policy alternatives the Egyptian government was faced with, particularly during the early phases of the reform process. This could be understood as a form of determination in the first instance on the part of the international. However, the second trend somehow counters this, as it shows that through a series of delays, selective implementations and sometimes actual 'hybridisation' of reforms, the national scale was still able to influence the timing, sequencing and as time went on also the content of reforms. *Pace* Schlumberger and other scholars arguing for the manipulation of economic processes for political purposes, this does not mean that the reforms implemented were not neoliberal anymore. In fact, if one is to accept that the 2011 revolution did not occur into a vacuum but rather had some socio-economic preconditions, then the argument of the neutralisation of reforms on the part of the ruling bloc loses most of its validity. Indeed, the interaction of these two trends suggests that there was a significant differentiation in the form of neoliberalism as it unfolded in Egypt compared to the template promoted by IFIs, international donors and investors during the 1990s. More specifically, neoliberalism in Egypt privileged the dimension of dispossession over that of competition and efficiency, and at times this meant resorting to unorthodox policies.

DOI: 10.1057/9781137395924

What does this tell us about hegemony? Certainly the decision to stop indulging in practices of dilatory reform and engage in a process of more thorough economic restructuring suggests that there had been a realisation of the increasing inability on the part of regime to deliver satisfactory economic results, and to diffuse them sufficiently, in order to obtain the support, or at least the acquiescence, of subaltern groups. In other words, it had become clear that there was an incipient hegemonic crisis on the national scale that needed tackling. At the same time, the institutional focus characteristic of this chapter has allowed us to only get a glimpse of the distributional effects of reforms. Getting to a more systematic understanding of the winners and losers of reforms, both within the regime and in society at large, is the task of the next chapter, which in turn gives us the chance to provide some deeper social content both to the hegemonic crisis of the Mubarak regime and the attempts to reconstruct authoritarian rule.

Notes

1   More specifically, Law 203 of 1991 concerning the privatisation of state-owned enterprises in the manufacturing sector, Law 95 and 96 of 1992 regulating respectively the capital market and land tenancy, and Law 88 of 2003 redefining the policy remit and functions of the central bank.

2   Two considerations are in order here. Firstly, at the risk of losing some of the complexities inherent in the currently globalising yet not entirely global political economy, global and international scale are considered as synonymous for purpose of this study. This is also consistent with Gramsci's use of the corresponding two Italian terms – *globale* and *mondiale* – as synonyms. Secondly, this study prefers the phrase 'spatial scales' to the classical 'levels of analysis' typical of mainstream IR and IPE. This is because the former is more precise than the latter in accounting for the necessary connection between different spatialities, as levels can be separated from one another (and indeed often are), whereas the relation with other configurations of territorial organisation – international, national, regional, local – is constitutive of the concept of scale.

3   Estimated as about LE21 billion for the fiscal years 2004/05 and 2005/06 (EIU 2006: 25) and LE 14 billion for 2006/07. The privatisation of Bank of Alexandria alone in June 2006 brought more than LE11 into the state coffers.

4   It was not possible to retrieve the data regarding 2006, the year of the privatisation of Bank of Alexandria. Separate data for joint-venture and

DOI: 10.1057/9781137395924

private banks became available only after 2004, after the entry into force of the new central banking law changed bank classification criteria.

5   Interviews with officials at the EU delegation in Egypt, Cairo, June 2010.

6   Every six months LCHR issues a report on land disputes occurred in Egypt. The numbers above are the sums of the data provided in these reports. They can accessed from the LCHR website: http://212.12.226.70/indexe.htm (1st access on 15 April 2010).

7   According to the EIU (1994), Mubarak and the ministers in direct contact with the IMF used repeatedly the argument that remittances constituted a greater source of foreign exchange earnings than exports.

8   Interview with CBE official, Cairo, June 2010.

9   Interview with Mahmoud Mohieldin, then minister of investment, Cairo, 4 July 2010.

10   He covered this position for the whole period between 1986 and 2004, while also being deputy prime minister for significant parts of this spell. In other words, Wali was one of the most important Egyptian policy-makers during the Mubarak era.

11   Interview with economist at the Information and Decision Support Center, Cairo, 31st March 2010.

12   See the *Doing Business Report* website: http://www.doingbusiness.org/Reforms/ (1st access on 23 May 2010).

13   Interview with Mahmoud Mohieldin, then minister of investment, Cairo, 4 July 2010.

DOI: 10.1057/9781137395924

3

Of Success and Greed: The New Business Class Turns into Capitalist Oligarchy

Abstract: *This chapter focuses on the distributional consequences of economic reforms in Egyptian society, showing how an entrepreneurial elite managed to amass an outstanding amount of wealth, and to translate it successfully in political power. However, the attempt at consolidating authoritarian rule under new economic foundations – what is termed here neoliberal authoritarianism – was likely to fail from its outset. This is because of the discontent created both within regime and in society at large by the rise of the capitalist oligarchy.*

Keywords: distribution of costs and benefits; neoliberal authoritarianism; capitalist oligarchy; informal practices; Gamal Mubarak

Roccu, Roberto. *The Political Economy of the Egyptian Revolution: Mubarak, Economic Reforms and Failed Hegemony*. Basingstoke: Palgrave Macmillan, 2014. DOI: 10.1057/9781137395924.

This chapter asks the '*cui bono*' question at the heart of any work in political economy (Strange 1988), thus attempting to understand which social groups benefitted the most from the neoliberal reforms implemented in the 1990s and 2000s. More specifically, the distributional impact of reforms is analysed in both its macro- and micro-effects. The former should put us in the position to assess which sectors of society saw their relative position improve or worsen because of reform, whereas the latter allows us to track down whether reforms empowered some business groups significantly more than others, and whether this might have had any consequences in relations between the different components supporting the Mubarak regime. This approach should thus enable us to evaluate whether any major frictions had emerged within the ruling bloc and between the regime and society at large. If the answer is positive, then the constellation of alliances and conflicts providing the background to the Egyptian revolution might start to emerge.

Moving beyond the institutional focus of the previous chapter, here the attention is turned on the broader relation between economic and political actors and factors. Given the widely acknowledged role of informality in Middle Eastern economic and political systems, an exclusive focus on institutional dynamics would most likely encounter severe difficulties in uncovering the articulations of economic and political forces. For this reason, this chapter focuses on both institutional and informal channels by which economic transformation might have produced also a reconfiguration of political power. On the one hand, the analysis of formal relations serves the purpose of highlighting what sort of changes have taken place in the balance of power between and within different institutions in the state apparatus. On the other hand, the additional focus on informal channels allows us to uncover the dynamics by which a new business class emerged as neoliberal reforms unfolded, and how this business class gradually managed to also amass considerable amount of power in the political arena.

In attempting to account for both institutional and informal dynamics, process-tracing is used extensively in this chapter. With its emphasis on the different micro-causal mechanisms leading to a given aggregate outcome, process-tracing allows us to assess the three main claims advanced in this chapter: firstly, that neoliberalism significantly strengthened the private entrepreneurial elite, both *vis-à-vis* other components of the regime and in society at large; secondly, that out of the two sections of the 'big capital' who benefited the most – the *infitah* bourgeoisie and

DOI: 10.1057/9781137395924

the new business class – only the latter took a more activist political stance attempting to translate its economic wealth not only in political influence, but rather in direct access to political office; thirdly, that the political rise of the business class and its eventual transformation into a capitalist oligarchy with strong predatory tendencies reinforced the neoliberal path undertook by the Egyptian economy, thus contributing in a major way to the further polarisation of relations both within the regime and in society at large. These three claims are assessed referring to descriptive statistics concerning wealth distribution but also for instance direct participation of businessmen in policy-making, analysis of existing secondary sources on the weight of informal relations in Egyptian politics, as well as interviews conducted with policy-makers and local experts, including both academics and journalists, which provide the chance to develop some short profiles of important businessmen and technocrats, whose rise (and sometimes fall) is deemed representative of the general process of empowerment of the new business class.

In the attempt of substantiating the three claims above, the chapter proceeds in the following way. The first section focuses on the mechanisms by which the Egyptian private sector, in both the *infitah* and new business class component, managed to accumulate a truly sizeable amount of wealth during the two decades of neoliberal reforms. The second section looks more specifically at the new business class, and at the channels by which it managed to translate its economic resources into direct political power, before discussing the consequences of the increased political role of this specific section of the ruling bloc. The third section instead assesses how the main winners of the reform process attempted to consolidate authoritarian rule on new economic foundations, ultimately failing, as demonstrated by the 2011 revolution.

Wealth accumulation and concentration, old and new

Reforms aimed at downsizing the direct role of the state in the economy did unsurprisingly play in the hands of the Egyptian private sector. Not all of it, though, as micro, small and medium enterprises often found themselves unable to cope with the combination of increased competition brought about by liberalisation and the byzantine procedures still characteristic of the Egyptian bureaucracy (El Mahdi and Rashed 2009). As a consequence, most of these companies found themselves

DOI: 10.1057/9781137395924

drifting towards informality, which can hardly be enlisted among the positive consequences of economic reforms (Elasrag 2010). However, large companies and business conglomerates benefitted handsomely from privatisations and liberalisations, leading for the first time since the nationalisations carried out by Nasser in 1956 and 1960–61 to the emergence of an indigenous business class not entirely dependent on the regime. It is possible more specifically to identify two sections of Egyptian private capitalists who managed to increase significantly their wealth during the two decades of reform: on the one hand, the bourgeoisie effectively created by Sadat with his *infitah*; on the other hand, a new business class often with strong links to Gamal Mubarak. Short profiles of selected members of these two groups may help us get a sense of how wealth accumulation on the part of big national capital happened.

A history often told of quintessential *infitah* businessman is the one of Osman Ahmed Osman (Sadowski 1991: 111–6; Mitchell 2002: 282). He opened up an engineering company in 1949, before King Farouk's overthrow, and was able to retain the managerial control of the company despite its formal nationalisation by Nasser and to establish a close friendship with Sadat, to the point of serving as minister of housing in the late 1970s. During *infitah*, Osman succeeded in expanding significantly the reach of its company beyond its original remit, and his main construction arm – Arab Contractors – was one of the largest companies in the Middle East and Africa until the 1980s, and still employs over 60,000 workers. In those years, Osman was also one of the first Egyptian businessmen to enter into the joint ventures with foreign capital now allowed by Law 43 of 1974. More specifically, exploiting a provision whereby public sector companies entering into joint ventures with foreign capital could be treated as private companies, Osman negotiated a deal with Pepsico and entered the most lucrative business that Egyptian agriculture could provide: land reclamation. Some of the consequences of the new legal status involved exemptions from price controls, independent budgeting authority, and most importantly the ability to retain profits instead of channelling them towards the treasury. Once Pepsico decided to sell its shares because of managerial divergences and administrative problems, Arab Contractors was ready to step in, becoming once more a public sector company and thus gaining access to subsidised loans, fuel and fertilisers.

Whereas Osman's rise is arguably unique because of the continuous trespassing of the private–public divide, it is still indicative of the ways in

DOI: 10.1057/9781137395924

which economic opening was managed in order to consolidate the position of the regime and of its main supporters. Somehow understandably, many of the families who had seen their fortunes rise during the *infitah* found themselves in an excellent position to also benefit from the 1990s and 2000s reforms. Invariably, in these occasions we are dealing with family dynasties, with one idolised founder and his (again, invariably) sons taking over and further expanding the business empire. A good example is the Bahgat family, with Ahmed skilfully exploiting free zones and investment incentives created by *infitah* to become the largest producer of TV sets in the Middle East. During 1990s, privatisations allowed his group to take over some state-owned enterprises (SOEs) and military production facilities which helped him upgrade his core business 'from assembling Korean sets to making Philips and own-name brands' (Mitchell 2002: 285). At the same time, he launched one of the most ambitious construction projects in Egypt's recent history, creating 'Dreamland', a luxury development meant to give a secluded shelter to the *nouveau riches* who could not cope anymore with life in hyper-congested Cairo (Mitchell 1999).

A similar story is the one of the Sawiris family, with their construction company Orascom becoming a giant in the Egyptian market in the aftermath of *infitah*. During the 1990s, the second generation headed by Naguib was quick to capitalise from the liberalisation and privatisation of telecoms, the first subsector in services to be reformed. Orascom Telecoms became the main local partner of the French company Orange in the first mobile operator in Egypt, MobiNil, and it soon also extended its reach overseas, mostly in other Middle Eastern and North African countries, but also venturing in Sub-Saharan Africa and acquiring in 2005 the third largest Italian mobile operator, Wind.

The Mohamed Mahmoud and the Mansour families provide further examples of building strength in a specific sector before extending business interests in ever larger parts of the national economy. The former began to operate during the times of the British occupation as a shoe-making workshop, before moving into the import and distribution of consumer goods and into the ever-thriving construction sector under *infitah*. As Mitchell put it (2002: 284), '[b]y the 1990s the group's thirteen companies included the MM chain of luxury fashion stores [...]; financial interests in the Egyptian Gulf Bank and the Pharaonic Insurance Company; the Datum internet service provider; the sole Egyptian agency for Jaguar cars; and showrooms selling motor vehicles from Rolls Royce

DOI: 10.1057/9781137395924

and Ferrari'. Import and sale of foreign cars, particularly for commercial purposes, was for long also the core business of the Mansour family, which in the 1990s also moved into tourism and internet technology.

The new generation of the Mansour family, represented by Mohamed Mansour, arguably constitutes the clearest link between the *infitah* bourgeoisie and the new business class emerging out of the 1990s reforms. Together with his cousin Ahmed Meghraby, Mohamed Mansour created the Palm Hills Development Company, one of the giants of tourism construction.

Because of his arrest and the widespread coverage of his trial, the best known member of the new business class revolving around Gamal Mubarak is certainly Ahmed Ezz, who succeeded in 'building up market leadership out of the blue' in the steel sector, controlling about 60 per cent of domestic steel production a mere decade away from the beginning of the privatisation process (Roll 2010: 356–357). Incidentally, during the process he also managed to use his prominent position within the NDP to get the dominant share held by a private company triggering anti-trust measures raised from 35 to 65 per cent. Other businessmen emerging during the phase of neoliberal reforms and personally connected to Gamal Mubarak include Rashid Mohammed Rashid, who served as president of Unilever North Africa, Middle East and Turkey, the regional branch of the multinational corporation, while keeping side interests in sectors as varied as food processing and finance, with a large stake in EFG-Hermes, one of the largest private banks in Egypt, through a joint-venture with the above-mentioned Mansour and Meghraby. In a way that distances them from the previous generation of businessmen, several members of this new business class spent a significant part of their lives abroad, often studying or working in the UK or the US.

These brief profiles allow us to make a couple of preliminary inferences regarding the political economy of reforms, and more specifically the highly uneven distribution of its benefits. Firstly, using a very apt phrase coined by Rex Brynen with reference to the Palestinian case (2000), here we are dealing with a 'very political economy', where strong links with prominent figures within the regime could guarantee a privileged path to the acquisition of profitable state-owned companies. Indeed, the correlation between being a member of the *infitah* bourgeoisie and enlarging your business empire through reforms in the 1990s and 2000s appears quite neat. Similarly, being a part of the club of 'Jimmy's boys' would most likely translate into a similar outcome.[1] In other words, politics

DOI: 10.1057/9781137395924

remained a key factor in determining the effect of economic reforms on your position in the social structure.

Secondly, it is not difficult to see how capital, being accumulated in such great amounts in so few hands, was – and still is – an extremely fungible resource in the Egyptian scenario, and thus could be deployed readily by those who had it in abundance in any given sector opened to private investment. This also had an impact on the composition of the Egyptian private sector. *Infitah* had created some private 'national champions' whose means of wealth accumulation were to be found almost exclusively in the import and sale of foreign products, in a function typical of the *comprador* bourgeoisie, and in the state-dependent construction sector, periodically boosted by public housing projects (Sims 2010). With the controlled opening of various sectors of the economy and the privileged access guaranteed to ruling bloc insiders, the profile of the Egyptian entrepreneurial elite was now more diversified, at the same time allowing for greater autonomy from the regime itself.

There are two main mechanisms by which the rise of these business groups took place. On the one hand, as already mentioned above, was the privatisation in the hands of private sector members of the ruling bloc. To be fair, these business groups were arguably the only Egyptian ones able to perform the capital-intensive functions usually required to run large-scale SOEs. Furthermore, the obsession with foreign economic interference which had survived the end of the Nasserist era still meant that domestic businessmen would be preferred as potential buyers for key SOEs. As it happened with the downsizing of PBDAC in agriculture, often the newly privatised companies would be put in the position of serving functions which were socially crucial, such as credit supply in countryside.

On the other hand, another powerful mechanism for the accumulation and concentration of wealth was the management of the reforming financial sector (Roll 2010). To begin with, the divestiture of state-owned shares in joint-venture banks significantly worsened the problem of credit concentration. According to the World Bank (2008: 26), in 2006 about 51 per cent of credit extended to the private sector went to only 0.19 per cent of clients. Banks clearly preferred lending to the few large corporations, with 30 of them accounting for about 40 per cent of total credit supply (Osman 2010: 115–6). At the same time, despite formal liberalisation, informal barriers to entry in the financial sector remained particularly high. In the banking sector, joint-ventures are still the main

DOI: 10.1057/9781137395924

way by which foreign banks can access the Egyptian market, as witnessed by the case of Crédit Agricole Egypt, whose entry was made possible only through an alliance with Mansour and Meghraby Investment and Development (MMID). Other than remaining undersized compared to the banking sector, capital markets also showed a marked dominance on the part of few Egyptian business groups. Indeed, the ownership structure of the main stock exchange index (EGX-30) in July 2010 showed how wealth was ever more concentrated in the hands of very few business groups, and ones which had very strong relations with the regime (see Table 3.1).

Thus, two extremely small groups of entrepreneurs constituting 'big capital' in Egypt had succeeded in amassing a truly astonishing amount of wealth, either in phases, as is the case for the *infitah* bourgeoisie, or much more rapidly, as with the new business class around Gamal. In a country where even the simplest economic activity appears to have a political connotation, one would inevitably expect such rise in the

TABLE 3.1   *Main business groups at EGX (2010)*

Company	Controlling shareholder	Market capitalisation (LE mn, 2008)	AmCham Top Ten (2009)	EGX 30 weight (%, July 2010)
Orascom Construction Industries	Sawiris	30,145	1	18.59
Orascom Telecom Holding	Sawiris	27,396	2	12.69
TMG Holding	Talaat Moustafa	6,212	6	6.47
Egyptian Company for Mobile Services (MobiNil)	Sawiris	14,686	3	4.23
Ezz Steel	Ezz	5,406	8	3.37
El Sewedy Cables	Sewedy	10,029	5	2.91
Palm Hills Development Company	Mansour, Meghraby	2,870	X	1.69
Egyptian for Tourism Resort	Kamel	2,017	X	0.89
Orascom Hotels Holding	Sawiris	1,809	X	Not included
Oriental Weavers Carpet Company	Khamis	1,738	X	Not included
Total	7 families	102,307 21.66%	6/10	50.84

Sources: EGX 2008 and 2010; AmCham 2010.

DOI: 10.1057/9781137395924

economic sphere to also have political consequences. If, as the late Samer Soliman put it (2011: 150), '[t]he distribution of political positions in Egypt obeys a precise equation that reflects the relative weight of various groups in the regime', then one would expect a rising number of businessmen attempting to influence policy-making. The next section shows that this was exactly the case.

The political rise of the new business class

Whereas the older generation of businessmen kept following the *infitah* strategy of reaping the benefits of reforms while steering away from the political arena, the new generation became increasingly active also in the latter. It is important to keep in mind that this analytical distinction between *infitah* and new capitalist class was not as clear-cut in reality as it might appear here. As mentioned above, Mohamed Mansour is arguably the best case in point to show how these two sections over-lapped to a good degree. One should similarly keep in mind that the army as such does not have direct economic interests only in the parallel economy it controls, but rather extends its interests also in the private sector, as privatisations allowed many members of the military, usually through their relatives, to become private entrepreneurs, in what Robert Springborg has aptly called 'Military Inc.'[2] However, I still maintain that the distinction proposed above is helpful in that it allows us to isolate a specific section of Egyptian large capital, outward-oriented and coa-lesced around Gamal Mubarak, which provided the domestic engine of neoliberalisation in the second decade of reforms.

There are two main institutional mechanisms providing for the politi-cal rise of the new business class and its transformation into a capitalist oligarchy. Firstly, there was a shift with respect to which ministries domi-nated decisions regarding the industrial sector. More specifically, the Ministry of Planning, a key institution for economic management during the *étatist* phase and historically characterised by a strong interventionist approach, was largely replaced by the Ministry of Trade and Industry, one of the most outward-oriented ministries (Soliman 2011: 131–135). This shift was even more evident in the customary practice under the Nazif cabinet to discuss economic policies within a smaller subset of ministers, called the Economic Group, dominated by the so-called *troika*: Youssef Boutros-Ghali for the Ministry of Finance, Mahmoud Mohieldin for the

DOI: 10.1057/9781137395924

Ministry of Investment, and the already mentioned Rashid Mohammed Rashid for the Ministry of Trade and Industry. While justified with reference to both competence of these individuals and the urgency of reforms needed, this removal of economic policy from collective cabinet discussions allowed to further marginalise *étatist* solutions, while at the same time some of its supporters were compensated with ministries of lesser economic relevance (Soliman 2011: 146).

The second institutional mechanism is an even more direct one, with businessmen becoming increasingly engaged into politics since the late 1990s in different capacities: as members of the ruling NDP, of parliament and of the cabinet. During the late 1990s, when the economy was dragged back into high deficit and low growth, the ruling party decided to widen its membership, and did so by attracting a younger generation of Egyptians who had been successful in the private sector. The role of catalyst played by Gamal Mubarak in the creation of this new section of the political class cannot possibly be overestimated (Collombier 2006: 8–10; Soliman 2011: 3). The party ranks were effectively beefed up with a number of businessmen in their thirties and forties, whose role within the party and in Egyptian politics at large increased significantly once Nazif was appointed prime minister in 2004.

A further advancement in this process would see these businessmen seeking direct political power, for example through election in parliament. This is exactly what happened, with the number of businessmen in parliament rising from 37 in 1995 to 77 in 2000 to 100 in 2005 (Soliman 2011: 145–6). The rise in numbers was accompanied by a rise in prestige, with big entrepreneurs violating a *domaine réservé* of bureaucrats and military officers such as the chairing of the Budget and Planning Committee, which was assigned in 2004 to Ahmed Ezz. At the same time, Gamal Mubarak became head of the party's Policies Secretariat.

The rise of the new business class led some of its members to enter directly into government, when Nazif appointed six businessmen to very prominent positions within his cabinet. For a start, the already discussed Rashid Mohammed Rashid became minister of trade and industry. Mohamed Mansour was appointed to head the Ministry of Transport, whereas Ahmed Meghraby, partner of the Mansour family in the Palm Hills Development Company, mostly active in construction and tourism, was unsurprisingly appointed first as minister of tourism and then minister of housing in a late 2005 cabinet reshuffle. Amin Abaza, one of the largest cotton traders in the country, became minister of agriculture,

DOI: 10.1057/9781137395924

and one of the greatest beneficiaries of the move from free towards 'cost-recovery' healthcare, Hatem El Ghabaly, was appointed to head the Ministry of Health and Population (Farah 2009).

Given the high stakes, it would be unrealistic to think that the political rise of this section of the capitalist class happened without a fight. And indeed, there was a great degree of opposition, particularly at the party level, against Gamal and his cohort of young – certainly by Egyptian standards – businessmen. This opposition was largely orchestrated by the so-called old guard (*al-haras al-qadim*), almost entirely composed by long-serving politicians and bureaucrats such as Zakaria Azmi, presidential chief of staff and one of Mubarak's closest advisors, and Safwat El-Sherif, the NDP's secretary general. These were supported in their attempt to resist the rise of the new business class by the upper echelons of the army, and particularly by Field Marshal Hussein Tantawi, minister of defence who would be called to head the Supreme Council of the Armed Forces (SCAF) in the transitional phase between Mubarak's fall and Morsi's election. The Eight NDP Congress held in 2002 proved to be the moment in which the change of the guard became apparent, with the new business class effectively gaining the upper hand in the ruling party, a transformation which would have momentous consequences for Egyptian politics and political economy as a whole.[3]

As suggested by Soliman's statement above, the political rise of a social group following its economic rise was not an uncommon event in Egyptian recent history. Something similar had already happened with the increasing presence of landlords in parliament since the 1970s, which allowed them to influence the formulation of agricultural policies in such a way as to exclude peasants (Bush 2000: 244). As part of his populist social contract, in the 1960s Nasser decreed that half the seats of the People's Assembly had to be reserved to the lower classes, with an electoral reform providing that each district would elect two MPs, one being either an industrial worker or a peasant and the other a professional or an official. While this provision was never formally repealed, already under Sadat seats reserved for peasants had been monopolised by the wealthiest of them or by clients of notables, to the point that when the 1992 tenancy law was issued, '[t]he parliament that approved the law did not contain one tenant' (Saad 2002: 106). This allowed large landowners to frame the issue of land reform according to their concerns not only in parliament, but also in the wider public discussion, with tenants being 'collectively accused of laziness, of spending too much

DOI: 10.1057/9781137395924

on entertainment and of enjoying the benefits of cheap rents while not increasing productivity' (Bush 2007: 1606). Similar forms of pressure, this time against a comprehensive tax reform and for the imposition of a General Sales Tax, was carried out by professional associations such as the American Chamber of Commerce in Egypt (AmCham) and the Egyptian Businessmen's Association (EBA) (Soliman 2011: 110–11).

The increased presence of businessmen in key positions of the political system was compounded by the appointment of technocrats with strong neoliberal credentials to even more vital positions for the reform process. Indeed, Youssef Boutros Ghali as minister of finance and Mahmoud Mohieldin as minister of investment were undoubtedly among the main drivers of the second wave of reforms starting in 2004. After a career at the IMF, Boutros Ghali served as advisor to the CBE governor. He was the youngest member of the team that negotiated ERSAP with the IMF and the World Bank. During the 1990s he started to cover ministerial posts and came under attack from the *étatist* wing within the NDP at the time of the 2000 parliamentary elections because of his neoliberal views. In these elections, Boutros Ghali was forced to run in a district other than his own against a strong opposition candidate, forcing him to a run-off to confirm his seat in the People's Assembly. In an interview with Oliver Schlumberger, an advisor close to the president said: 'His plans for reform come too early for Egypt. So we had to show him: "we can kill you like we made you" ' (2004: 121). In the matter of a few years, however, it appeared that his economic plans had come of age, leading to his appointment to the position of finance minister under Nazif.

On the other hand, Mahmoud Mohieldin read economics at Cairo University, the quintessential institution for studying the subject in Egypt and one with very close ties to the regime.[4] He then moved to the UK to get a Master's degree at York and a PhD in economics at Warwick. Once back in Egypt in the mid-1990s, he started lecturing at Cairo University and was involved from the very outset in the creation and management of the Egyptian Center for Economic Studies, one of the leading think tanks in the country. At the same time, he began his rise at the party level, co-chairing the NDP's Economic Committee and becoming one of the strongest critics of the 'illiberal policies' carried out by the Ebeid cabinet, and waging a battle – discussed in greater depth in the following chapter – that led to the dismissal of the cabinet and the appointment of a new one with Nazif as prime minister and Mohieldin himself heading the newly created Ministry of Investment.

DOI: 10.1057/9781137395924

The increased penetration of prominent businessmen and technocrats had a significant effect on policy-making too, in that it led to a remarkable acceleration on the reform path. The economic rise followed by a political rise created a positive feedback loop for the new business class, which would speed up the implementation of the sort of policies that allowed its rise in the first place. At the same time, given that this rise was anything but uncontroversial, the decision to proceed on such a path regardless of opposition within the ruling bloc and in broader society, together with the tendency towards the cannibalisation of key economic and political positions, made this new business class ever more similar to a capitalist oligarchy, ruling in its own exclusive interest and predating the country's resources along the way. This was clearly a risky path, both with respect to relations within the regime and between the regime and society at large.

Constructing neoliberalism authoritarianism on shaky ground

The winner-take-all approach of the new business class inevitably posed a serious challenge to the carefully constructed balance of social forces within the regime. As brilliantly put by Ayubi (1995: 352), the *infitah* bourgeoisie had been effectively created by the regime and introduced into the ruling bloc as long as it would play the role of 'junior partner' of the army, which would remain the uncontested majority stakeholder in the regime. Reforms in the 1990s and 2000s went a long way in emancipating the private sector component of the regime from the army. However, we have seen that not all sections of large private capital in Egypt participated to the occupation and domination of the political sphere. So, what was the position of the emerging capitalist oligarchy *vis-à-vis* other sections of large private capital and most importantly the army?

The relative position of the different fractions of the Egyptian capitalist class can be measured referring to a set of parameters proposed by Luciani for evaluating the independence of the national bourgeoisie from the regime in the Middle East (2007: 287–8, ft. 9). He suggests that five indicators should be taken into account: accumulated wealth, access to global finance and know-how, competitiveness and profitability of enterprises, independence from government protection,[5] and sales to

DOI: 10.1057/9781137395924

market as opposed to sales to government. Both the *infitah* bourgeoisie and the new business class score extremely high on the first indicator, possibly with the *infitah* business dynasties still richer than the new generation, which instead appears to score higher on the second indicator because of its closer links with global capital. On the third indicator, whilst large enterprises were certainly profitable, it is difficult to single out the ones that were so because of their competitiveness, particularly considering the conditions of domestic quasi-monopoly in which they often operated. Extra-profits made in the domestic market could then be used to promote exports abroad, thus looking at exports too might provide a misleading assessment of which companies are more competitive. Neither of the two sections of large private capital however could be said to be entirely independent from government, and this is particularly evident with respect to the persisting importance of political connections to accumulate wealth, which arguably outweighs the decreasing role of the state as a prominent buyer of goods and services produced by the private sector. Once again contrary to the predictions of modernisation and democratisation theory, the opening up of the economy did produce a stronger business class, but one that was not significantly more independent from the regime than its predecessor. Furthermore, whereas the army might have been relatively weakened by reforms, it could still count on the parallel military economy, estimated to be worth between 25 and 35 per cent of the country's GDP (Jadaliyya 2013).

If these were the conditions within which Egyptian private capital operated, the most rational choice for the new business class would have been to improve their position within the existing regime, and possibly shift its economic foundations further away from *étatism*, but at the same time avoiding a full-fledged democratisation. At the end of the day, economic benefits were accruing to them in great amounts, and political opening might have meant that groups excluded from the ruling bloc could get a voice in decision-making, potentially putting at risk the position of the entrepreneurial elite within the reformed political economy. Thus, the goal was arguably to further shift the policy platform in a neoliberal direction, from which they would benefit because of the uneven distribution of benefits guaranteed by their position within the regime, without endangering the survival of the regime itself, ultimate guarantor of the politico-economic order.

Whereas developments on the formal and institutional level saw the neoliberal agenda and its proponents becoming ever more prominent, it

DOI: 10.1057/9781137395924

is mostly through informal mechanisms that the attempt at reorganising authoritarian rule took place. This is particularly evident in financial sector reforms, which combined a strong emphasis on attracting foreign investors with the unwillingness to tackle the major inefficiencies related to easy and unscrutinised lending on the part of public sector banks towards both state-owned and private businesses. Under Mohieldin, the government carried out an aggressive campaign in order to reduce non-performing loans (NPLs), that is, loans never paid back. On paper the reform was extremely successful, as it managed to get NPLs as a share of total gross loans from 24 to 15 per cent between 2004 and 2008 (World Bank 2010a). This reduction was achieved by adopting a more flexible approach to debt settlement, managed by a special unit within CBE allowing banks and debtors to reach deals without going to court. Whereas this may appear a sensible approach, as it improved banking sector performance without overburdening the judiciary, it also led to a further lack of transparency that benefitted large debtors, more often than not corresponding to large businesses, both private and public (Roll 2010: 357–8). Thus, this procedure allowed the government to win the IFIs' praise while at the same time benefitting the various components of the ruling bloc at the expense of the state's coffers and thus of wider society.

More generally, neoliberal policies were combined with an attempt at reorganising authoritarian rule. On the one hand, the institution-alisation of neoliberalism was visible in the empowerment of the more outward-oriented ministries, from the Ministry of Trade and Industry to the Ministry of Investment, to the detriment of traditionally *étatist* insti-tutions. The increasing number of top political posts occupied by busi-nessmen and neoliberal economists significantly reinforced this trend. On the other hand, the survival of pre-existing informal practices, from a less than transparent management of privatisations to skewed access to credit in favour of large companies to the NPLs settlement procedures mentioned above, helped in reconciling the shift in economic policies with the preservation of authoritarian rule.

And who better than Gamal Mubarak, the president's son but also the undoubted leader of the neoliberal wing, could embody this attempt at turning around the Egyptian economy while restabilising political rule? While potentially constituting this quintessential link between two generations and two ways of managing the Egyptian political economy, Gamal came to be increasingly perceived by the army as 'the other', in

DOI: 10.1057/9781137395924

a *crescendo* of suspicions and back-stabbing that arguably harmed the survival prospects of the regime nearly as much as popular protests.

Other than worsening relations between the main components of the ruling bloc, the combination of institutional and informal mechanisms also produced a dramatic increase in inequality in broader society. This has been confirmed by the World Bank, which in an analysis of the latest Household Income, Expenditure and Consumption Survey (HIECS) shows that the absolute poverty ratio increased from 16.7 per cent in 2000 to 19.6 in 2005. If one also takes into account what the World Bank defines as 'near poverty',[6] the total number of the poor goes over 40 per cent. Increasing protests, both in the countryside and in the factories, also suggest that lower classes were largely excluded from the benefits of reforms visible in remarkably healthy rates of aggregate growth, averaging about 6 per cent between 2004 and 2008. Probably even more interestingly, social groups between the elites and the traditional poor, what Leonard Binder called 'the second stratum' (1978), appear on the whole to have been weakened by neoliberal reforms. Thus, the squeezing of the Egyptian middle class, particularly in its largest section made up of public sector employees, together with the worsening conditions of the working classes, be they industrial, rural or informal, suggested that threats for regime survival might not come exclusively from intra-regime frictions, but rather from increasing pressures from below. The January 2011 revolution would prove that this was the case.

Conclusion

The emergence and at the same time the precariousness of neoliberal authoritarianism can best be understood once we look at the interaction between economic and political actors and factors through the method of articulation. More specifically, this chapter has seen how an exercise of political agency – that is, the decision to undertake far-reaching economic reforms along a neoliberal path – produced structural change in terms of a shift towards a new accumulation regime, which in turn led to significant modifications in the class structure, with more profits accruing to large private capital, less revenues entering into the state coffers, and real wages deteriorating considerably. This structural change in turn redefined the boundaries within which political agency could take place, significantly empowering the social groups made better off by the shift,

DOI: 10.1057/9781137395924

and weakening the remaining ones. Here the relative autonomy of the political is still visible in the attempt on the part of the main components of the ruling bloc to articulate the emerging neoliberal economic order with pre-existing practices that would safeguard the survival of authoritarian rule.

After all, articulatory practices often aim at relating seemingly contradictory features. This is even more so in pre-capitalist or newly capitalist societies, where the political enjoys a higher degree of autonomy from the class structure, providing more room for the survival of old practices alongside a new accumulation regime. As Ayubi put it, '[i]t is a distinct advantage of the articulation method that it would enable us to conceive of a situation where the "technical" arrangements most typical of a particular mode of production may be articulated with the cultural (and political) aspects more typical of another mode (and therefore possibly of another "age")' (1995: 29). This also applies within capitalism, and thus with the shift from a regime of capital accumulation to another. And this is what we saw in the Egyptian case: a move from an *étatist* to a neoliberal accumulation regime, producing substantial modifications in relations between class forces, but still being articulated by political agents with pre-existing practices aiming at the preservation of authoritarian rule under new economic foundations.

This process of hybridisation of neoliberalism is not to be seen necessarily as a move away from its original nature. Indeed, as already discussed in the previous chapter, the Egyptian case displays most of the typical features of neoliberalised economies. Among these, the most relevant are the rise in inequality, the increasing polarisation in society between a 'super-rich' class and weakened middle and lower classes, and the rise of the financial sector that in Egypt instead of becoming dominant as in Anglo-Saxon economies works more as the cement linking together the different forms of capital and thus allowing the ever greater fungibility of the latter. The social effects of these characteristic features of neoliberalism were arguably even worsened by the articulation with pre-existing aspects of the Egyptian political economy, from its dependent position in the global economy and the sustained dominance of domestic over foreign capital discussed in the previous chapter to persisting practices of corruption, patronage and crony capitalism, which effectively confirm the hypothesis of differential integration advanced by Halliday (2002).

This lopsided transformation of the Egyptian political economy appeared to be creating increasing tensions both within the regime and

DOI: 10.1057/9781137395924

in society at large. Here is where hegemony comes back to the fore. To be successful hegemony has by definition to be encompassing, including social groups beyond the ruling bloc. In other words, it is the task of the latter, and within it of the dominant and/or rising fraction, to develop a 'conception of the world' of which most groups feel part of, regardless of their position in society. Establishing whether the neoliberal project carried out by the new business class was also a hegemonic one is the task of the next chapter.

Notes

1   Currently used almost entirely in a derogatory way, Jimmy seems to have been the name by which Gamal was usually called within his own family, under the influence of his half-Welsh mom Suzanne.

2   *Egypt Independent*, 26 October 2011, available online at http://www. egyptindependent.com/news/us-expert-leadership-military-inc-running-egypt (1st access on 29 October 2011).

3   Given that the party congress was the moment in which power and ideas were mobilised to a great extent in a battle that would significantly alter the relations of force within the ruling bloc and in society at large, this specific event is analysed in greater depth in the following chapter.

4   In his bestselling novel *The Yacoubian Building*, Alaa Al Aswany provides a very vivid description of the elitism of FEPS (Faculty of Economics and Political Science) students: 'For some reason, the Faculty of Economics and Political Science at Cairo University is associated in people's minds with affluence and chic. Its students, if asked in which faculty they are in, are accustomed to reply: "Economics and Political Science" in a complacent, confident, and nonchalant way (as though saying, "Yes, indeed. We are, as you can see, the tops")' (2007: 89).

5   Luciani proposes government subsidies as a more specific indicator. However, considering the range of methods through which the government was able to support and/or control the local capitalist class in Egypt, I consider the broader conception of protection to be more appropriate than an exclusive focus on subsidies.

6   In the same report, the World Bank defines poverty as 'spending less than needed to cover absolutely minimal food and non-food costs', whereas 'near poverty' is defined as 'spending barely enough to meet basic food and slightly more than essential non-food needs' (2007: ii).

DOI: 10.1057/9781137395924

4

Ideology Resurgent? Neoliberalism as Economic–Corporate Project for the Few

Abstract: *Through a focus on the main economic think tanks and the 2002 congress of the ruling party, this chapter discusses how neoliberalism increasingly became a guide for economic policy-making. However, the failure of neoliberalism to penetrate into wider society witnesses the inability on the part of the new business class to go beyond the 'economic–corporate moment' and fulfil its hegemonic potential.*

Keywords: neoliberalism; ideology; hegemony; organic intellectuals; economic-corporate moment

Roccu, Roberto. *The Political Economy of the Egyptian Revolution: Mubarak, Economic Reforms and Failed Hegemony*. Basingstoke: Palgrave Macmillan, 2014. DOI: 10.1057/9781137395924.

A Gramscian approach based on articulation can also shed light on a third dimension of the political economy of reforms in Egypt, and to how these contributed to the unravelling of the Mubarak regime. Whereas the previous two chapters focused respectively on the interaction along the international–national and economic–political spheres, this chapter discusses the respective role of material forces and ideas, and most importantly of their interactions, in producing the neoliberal turn experienced by the Egyptian economy. An approach along these lines has a theoretical and two empirical payoffs. In theoretical terms, it allows this work to eschew instrumentalist explanations that see ideas as merely functional to a specific economic and political project, as well as constructivist accounts that tend to detach the role of ideas as the main driving force of such a project from the social forces promoting those very ideas. In empirical terms, this approach allows on the one hand to show how neoliberalism gradually became the dominant discourse with respect to economic policy-making thanks to the pressures on the part of specific actors, and more specifically of the capitalist oligarchy, whose profile has been outlined in the previous chapter. On the other hand, it provides the chance to assess the performative power of neoliberalism but also its limitations, mostly in its failure to provide a discourse that would penetrate from policy-making circles into wider society.

The evaluation of these arguments is complicated in the Egyptian case by two peculiarities whose implications point in very different directions with respect to this articulation of material and ideational factors. On the one hand, as suggested by Babb (2001: 16–21), within an increasingly integrated global economy based on freedom of movement for capital and goods, developing countries are caught in a dilemma by which the more they open up their markets, the more they become resource-dependent. In turn, the growing importance of foreign capital also increases the sensitivity of national policy-makers to the demands of foreign companies and governments. As a consequence, resource dependence often translates into knowledge dependence, with policy-makers and academics being pushed to follow the wisdom of the day in the more powerful countries. This line of reasoning should apply in an even stronger way to the Egyptian economy, as reliant as it is on various forms of rent.

On the other hand, republican Egypt was born in a climate of strong rhetoric against the United States and the West under Nasser. Under Sadat, the *étatist* framework with respect to economic policy was not altered significantly by *infitah* (Waterbury 1983). The sedimentation of these ideational

DOI: 10.1057/9781137395924

aspects could not be wiped off overnight.[1] The transformation of 'common sense' as intended by Gramsci is always a molecular, and thus gradual, process. This argument would seem to suggest some form of path-dependence with respect to the cognitive paradigm guiding economic policy-making. While this is not necessarily opposed to the correlation between resource and knowledge dependence, it is safe to assume that the economic nationalist heritage acted as a countervailing force in the Egyptian case.

While attempting to weight in the relative importance of these two trends, this chapter focuses on the material and discursive causes and effects of the rise of neoliberalism in Egypt. In doing this, it proceeds in the following way. The first section discusses the social forces behind the emergence of the two most important economic think tanks in Egypt. The Gramscian concept of organic intellectuals is used to discuss how these think tanks, in conjunction with two business associations, performed the fundamental function of clarification, organisation and popularisation of the key ideas of the heart of the reform project advocated by the capitalist oligarchy. The second section focuses more specifically on the 2002 Congress of the ruling National Democratic Party, which constitutes the perfect case study for understanding how neoliberal concepts and ideas were mobilised in support of the political project of the faction around Gamal Mubarak against the *étatist* wing of the regime. The third section instead focuses on the ability of neoliberalism as a discourse to feed back on materiality, on the one hand by effectively reshaping the playing field against any form of state intervention in the economy and in favour of the emerging capitalist oligarchy, and on other hand by encouraging a predatory behaviour on the part of the latter which created major frictions both within the regime and in relations between the new business class and the rest of Egyptian society. The concluding section tries to understand how the material and discursive limits of neoliberalism might have adversely affected regime stability, which was to be proved much more apparent than actual.

Manufacturing consent for neoliberalism: think tanks as organic intellectuals

As discussed in Chapter 2, the participation of Egyptian actors to the design of policies during the first years of structural adjustment was

DOI: 10.1057/9781137395924

limited to either accepting, rejecting or delaying the implementation of measures promoted by IFIs. This largely reactive attitude suggests that in this first phase the main driver of Egyptian economic policies was the need to comply, mostly in order to obtain debt forgiveness and rescheduling on the part of Paris Club countries. With respect to the wider public sphere, in fact, free market ideas did not have much currency. Rather, the main public intellectuals, such as for example Galal Amin, tended to rely on a form of economic nationalism that combined some elements of the Nasserist project with the state-led developmentalist model provided by East Asian tigers. In this respect, the economic policy debate in Egypt was not significantly different from what could be seen in other developing countries with an *étatist* tradition, such as Mexico, before the rise of the 'money doctors' that through tighter fiscal and monetary policies disciplined the local state, effectively laying down the groundwork for a shift towards neoliberalism (Babb 2005).

In the Egyptian case a similar shift was accompanied and facilitated by the work of the two most important economic think tanks, both created in the early 1990s. The Economic Research Forum was from its inception a region-wide research centre, covering the whole Arab world, but also Iran and Turkey. Most of its donors were, and still are, foreign foundations and institutions, including the Ford Foundation, which contributed $1 million to the original endowment fund, the United Nations Development Programme (UNDP), the World Bank, the EU-funded FEMISE (*Forum Euroméditerranéen des Instituts des Sciences Économiques*), and the Arab Fund for Economic and Social Development. The tendency of the Ford Foundation to finance research programmes that would cast the issue of political development in Third World countries in a way that was conducive, and indeed subordinate, to the creation of free markets has already been analysed in the literature (Cammack 1997). Although for different reasons, also the other international and regional institutions financing ERF have been criticised for their reductivist understanding of economics as a science, usually simply conflated with the neoclassical synthesis, which would in turn suggest that development is best achieved following the principles of the Washington Consensus, or at best of the 'Washington Consensus augmented' (Rodrik 2006). At the same time, broader geographical focus and international sponsorship allowed the ERF to be removed from the debate on Egyptian economic policy, thus reducing the influence of the various components of the regime. This in turn had two further consequences. Firstly, most of the academic

DOI: 10.1057/9781137395924

production was not immediately policy-relevant, from the working paper series to the recently launched semestral publication, *Middle East Development Journal*. Secondly, as outlined above, heavy reliance on external funds translated into a tendency to employ economic models prevalent on the international scale.

The establishment of ECES has a very different story. It was established in 1992 by the various components of the Egyptian business community exactly with the aim of being policy-relevant. Representatives from the largest companies in the most relevant sectors of the economy were represented on the ECES board, including food processing (Rashid Mohammed Rashid and Shafiq Boghdady), textiles (Mohammed Khamis and Galal Zorba), electronics (Ahmed Bahgat), car industry (Mohamed Mansour), steel production (Ahmed Ezz), banks (Adel El Labban for the Commercial International Bank), as well as local representatives of global consultancy firms such as Mackenzie and KPMG. Most importantly, Gamal Mubarak was also a member of the ECES board. Given the board composition, it should not come as a surprise that by the late 1990s ECES had become the centre where the policy platform of the 'reformist' wing of the ruling bloc was elaborated, under the theoretical leadership of Mahmoud Mohieldin, then senior economist at ECES and advisor of Youssef Boutros Ghali at the Ministry of Economy. The careful reader will have noticed that several of these names already appeared in the previous chapter, as prominent members of the new business class turned into a capitalist oligarchy. In this respect, looking at ECES means analysing the 'brain' of the neoliberal wing within the NDP. Indeed, Frederik Richter epitomised the role of ECES in the clearest possible way, suggesting that its main task was 'to formalise the NDP's economic policies and to feed private sector promotion with macro-economic expertise based on an IMF and World Bank oriented thinking' (2006).

The work of ERF and ECES was complemented on a more accessible level by *Business Monthly*, the magazine published by AmCham. With its 'fact-filled' articles about new investment opportunities brought about by economic reforms, *Business Monthly* was extremely successful in popularising the emerging neoliberal wisdom, while at the same time creating an *esprit de corps* in the newly emerging section of the Egyptian business community.[2] Through the conjunction of these two functions of divulgation and socialisation, AmCham played a fundamental role in the creation and diffusion of a neoliberal 'common sense' among the local capitalist class.

DOI: 10.1057/9781137395924

Whereas the division of labour between these organisations was not necessarily planned nor intended, their actual function can still be captured by the Gramscian concept of *organic intellectuals*, which accounts for the powerful role of ideas in shaping material changes without forsaking their link to specific interests grounded in social relations of production. Gramsci defines organic intellectuals as 'intellectuals by social function' arising from a specific group, with the task of clarifying and organising the interests and ideology of their social class, or fraction thereof (Gramsci 1971: 6, 330). Once elaborated into a relatively coherent cultural, political and economic programme, this ideology becomes operative and produces substantive effects also on material conditions.

Organic intellectuals are most successful when they are able to articulate the ideology of the social group they belong to in a way that is consistent with existing common sense, and indeed penetrates into it. Thus, organic intellectuals are required to perform two vital functions in the challenge to an existing hegemony and the construction and reproduction of an alternative one. On the one hand, they are expected to provide solid theoretical grounding to the interests of the class or class fraction they belong to, which in turn will also lead to a clarification of these very interests and thus the emergence of a more coherent policy agenda to achieve them. On the other hand, organic intellectuals must also do a work of divulgation and popularisation, allowing their ideology to be articulated with the existing common sense and thus become hegemonic within society.

Thus, it is certainly not enough to show the relevance of material funding in setting up ERF and ECES to suggest we are dealing with the organic intellectuals of the new business class. To ascertain whether this is the actual function these organisations played, one should also find how their activity clarified, organised and gave scientific credibility to the reform agenda of the new business class. This is done by looking at how neoclassical economics became ever more prominent in both the ERF and ECES working paper series, with the consequence of redefining the boundaries of what is deemed to be 'respectable' economics.[3] This aim was achieved through a process of depoliticisation of economic policy-making, portrayed as a technical field best left to the decisions of economic experts. Increasing reliance on neoclassical economic models and theories was instrumental in reshaping the boundaries of social action, by reframing what 'the economy' is, how it should be treated as

DOI: 10.1057/9781137395924

an 'object' of study, and what are the desirable outcomes that economic policies should pursue. More specifically, the aim of economists and economic policy-makers was reshaped in terms of welfare maximisation, leading to the 'growth fetishism' much criticised by Galal Amin and effectively expunging issues of inequality and redistribution, considered as social rather than actual economic problems.

The ideology of the new capitalist class was also reinforced by foreclosing potential debates about alternative policy avenues. Around the turn of the century, the potential tension of an export-led strategy that simultaneously called for a retreat of the state from industrial policy started to be debated by prominent academics in the light of the success of the East Asian model (Amin 2000; Abdel-Khalek 2001). A 2005 ECES paper put to rest the option of change in strategy, by suggesting that the East Asian model could not be reproduced elsewhere, and even less in the Middle East, because of its cultural specificity, and because it increased corruption and produced disincentives to skill development in the financial sector, and neither of these features was sustainable anymore in a world where capital mobility had become the starting assumption (Noland and Pack 2005). Interestingly, the last section of the paper collapsed its policy recommendations exactly into the 'Washington Consensus augmented', with suggestions framed under the lens of structural adjustment combined with bland considerations on the importance of institutional quality and human capital.[4]

A similar shift can be seen also with respect to trade liberalisation, where the role of the state had to be confined to the gradual but steady dismantlement of trade barriers exactly in order to foster an export-led industry. In a 2003 ECES working paper, Amal Refaat analysed the reduction of tariff barriers to manufactured goods between 1994 and 2002 without ever doubting the assumption that trade liberalisation had been inherently good for the Egyptian economy. This is particularly interesting, given that by then the most powerful indictment of the damaging effects of trade and price liberalisation on Egyptian manufacturing, in the form of Dutch disease and hence de-industrialisation, had already been published (Abdel-Khalek 2001). In this respect, one could see what cognitive scientists call confirmation bias, with the tendency to systematically discount both theoretical arguments and empirical data disconfirming one's conception of the world, its assumptions and the hypotheses derived thereof.

DOI: 10.1057/9781137395924

Thus, ERF and ECES certainly played the first function that is required of organic intellectuals, giving a theoretical grounding to the positions of the social group they represented, while at the same time thwarting any serious attempt to bring state direct intervention in the economy as a plausible option. When this happened, it was always coated in a logic of exception, justified by pressing extra-economic reasons. This is for example the way in which the restart of public provisions of fertilisers in the mid-1990s was justified (MEED 1997). The privatisation of input provision had been supported by reference to the crowding out thesis, according to which excessive state intervention was preventing private actors to enter these markets and more efficiently supply the same products. However, the application in practice of this principle proved disastrous. On the one hand, the downsizing of the PBDAC led to substantial credit shortage, thus decreasing the spending power particularly of medium and small farmers. On the other hand, privatisation in the provision of fertilisers produced the conditions for the emergence of a cartel that brought the prices of fertilisers well above what could be paid by most farmers (Bush 1999: 68–9). Thus, what the Egyptian agriculture was experiencing was a clear case of market failure, leading to waves of unrest in the countryside. Indeed, the reintroduction of public provision of fertilisers was in fact justified not on economic terms, but rather in terms of national security.

As suggested above, the clarification and systematic organisation of an ideology is only a first step towards its transformation into a new common sense for society at large. Because of the molecular nature of common sense, this is a long and ongoing process, where many attempts at the articulation of different – and sometimes contradictory – ideas take place over time, which even when successful are always prone to contestation and ultimately transformation. This uncertainty is further deepened by what Bruff calls the 'unstable anchoring' of ideas in society (2008: 56). At the same time, the consolidation of an ideology would certainly be facilitated by its practical success, that is, its ability to become a guide for changing the world (or leaving it as it is, for that matter). Towards this goal, some social groups have a strong interest in somehow stabilising the ever-shifting understanding of what is entailed by an ideology and bend it towards serving its own interests. This is exactly what Stuart Hall refers to as 'the moment of power' (1997: 30). And for understanding whether neoliberalism became the guide for economic policy-making in Egypt and was absorbed through divulgation and popularisation within

DOI: 10.1057/9781137395924

wider society, one must start from the political battle that undoubtedly signals a tidal change in the relations of force between the different components of the Mubarak regime.

The battle for ideas (and power): the 2002 NDP congress

Whereas the previous chapter has discussed how the Eight NDP Congress in 2002 produced a substantial change of personnel in power, with the political rise of the new business class, this section focuses more on the discursive construction of the neoliberal critique of the economic policies carried out by the Ebeid cabinet. This allows us to understand the power of economic ideas in unifying and mobilising different sections within the ruling party against the incumbent government, effectively providing the preconditions for its replacement in 2004 with the Nazif cabinet. At the same time, it also gives an idea of the role played by individual organic intellectuals in elaborating a 'new thinking' (*fikr al-jadid*) on economic policy, and thus suggesting an agenda that would attract different sections within the party.

By the end of the 1990s the impetus for reforms had withered away, held hostage of the power struggle within the NDP. On the one hand, the *étatist* wing saw public sector reform as a dangerous erosion of state power that might jeopardise social stability. On the other hand, the rising private sector component succeeded in portraying itself as 'reformist', thus casting the opposing faction as committed to preserve an unsustainable status quo. The 2002 NDP Congress provided the battleground where these two conceptions of the economic path to be followed squared off (Collombier 2006).

The discursive construction of an opposition between a reformist and a conservative faction in order to cast the incumbent Ebeid government under a negative light had two substantial discursive implications. On the one hand, by appropriating the general characterisation of 'reformist' to identify a specific instantiation of reforms, it foreclosed the room for the emergence of alternative reform projects. This applied not only towards other components of the ruling bloc, but also – and possibly more importantly – also with respect to other groups in society, as the qualification of 'reformist' came to have an entirely economic connotation, thus foreclosing the room for discussion of meaningful

DOI: 10.1057/9781137395924

reform – read: democracy – in the political sphere. On the other hand, as the self-styled reformist project relied so heavily on the marketisation of the Egyptian economy, it implicitly charged any form of public intervention in the economy that could not be seen as market-creating or market-conforming as conservative and thus unwilling to free national and international companies from the shackles imposed by Nasser's planned economy.

This second element is particularly visible in another recurrent discursive device: any attempt at maintaining some form of public control over market forces would be labelled as 'illiberal', and thus depicted as running against the natural order of things. This tendency was particularly visible in the attack to the policies in the banking sector adopted by the incumbent government, which during the Congress was attacked by Mahmoud Mohieldin and Sahar Nasr, both members of the party economic committee. In the first page of an ERF working paper they eloquently express the same case in less politically charged and allegedly scientific terms, even though the academic references given invariably belong to the hardcore neoclassical tradition. Because of this attempt to recast in neutral and technical terms what is essentially a political argument, this passage is worth quoting in full (2003: 1):

> [P]ublic ownership of banks tends to be associated with financial repression, poorly developed banking systems, higher interest rate spreads, slower financial development, and lower economic growth. Moreover, empirical evidence shows that public banks seemed to generate enormous losses that impose a huge burden on the economies. Such problems that are inherent in banking systems dominated by public ownership have led many countries to considering privatising their public banks. Experience has also shown that public banks can contribute to banking crises by permitting political objectives to distort market operations. [...] Public banks are more likely to allocate capital to low productivity investments. Moreover, public banks tend to have a lower incentive to identify problem loans, and to minimise costs.

Much as with 'illiberal', also the reference to the term 'repression' for any form of limitation of capital movement in the financial sector signals the creation of a discursively charged playing field, where some policy options are labelled in a way that seems to suggest their ethical undesirability. With such strong opinions on the issue of public ownership of banks, it should not surprise that once the neoliberal faction won the 2002 battle within the party, with Mohieldin as minister of

DOI: 10.1057/9781137395924

investment and Nasr as World Bank supervisor for the financial sector reform programme, the new government managed to divest virtually all public sector shares in joint-venture banks and to privatise Bank of Alexandria.

Indeed, the creation of an uneven discursive playing field also provided the basis for the alliance of the two main factions of opponents to the Ebeid cabinet. On the one hand, one could find what Abdel Moneim Said called 'the liberals with a past', including bureaucrats but also entrepreneurs in their fifties who had been supporters of both macroeconomic stabilisation and structural adjustment in the 1990s, but had seen their position within the regime weakened by the resurgence of the *étatist* component. The most important personality in this group was the already mentioned Youssef Boutros Ghali. On the other hand, the other main group attracted by Mohieldin's agenda was the one he was most directly related to, labelled by Moneim Said as 'the new "new guard"', led by Gamal Mubarak and including the new business tycoons (Collombier 2006: 9).

This alliance was particularly successful in marginalising the *étatist* faction within the ruling party, and the decisions taken at the end of the 2002 Congress witnessed this change of the tide. Mohieldin's appointment as co-chairman of the economic committee of the party showed the reformist wing taking control of the main forum for economic policy discussion. As mentioned in the previous chapter, in July 2004 the Ebeid government was replaced with one headed by Ahmed Nazif. Even more importantly, the composition of what was labelled the 'economic dream team' by the regime-controlled press demonstrated how this alliance of different generations united by a neoliberal outlook had become prominent (Cook 2012). Even though slightly older than the likes of Ahmed Ezz, Rashid Mohammed Rashid was the perfect embodiment of the new business class, with his links to global companies and his business interests in most strategic sectors of the Egyptian economy. Youssef Boutros Ghali, as said above, was instead the classical 'liberal with a past'. And Mahmoud Mohieldin, for whom a tailor-made ministry was created, had contributed in no small part to the provision of much needed theoretical and discursive glue holding together neoliberal technocrats with likeminded businessmen.

During the battle with the *étatist* faction, one of the most daunting challenges for the neoliberals was to reconcile their calls for wide-ranging economic reforms with regime stability. Whereas the presence of Gamal

DOI: 10.1057/9781137395924

himself should have provided some assurance in this respect,[5] there were also attempts to cast the reform agenda as a way of bolstering social peace, thus consolidating the position of the regime. This was done in two ways. On the one hand, worsening macroeconomic indicators under the Ebeid suggested that the strategy of tightly controlling integration in the global economy was preventing Egypt from garnering its potential benefits without providing a sufficient backstop against its deleterious effects, as witnessed by the shockwaves of the East Asian crisis. What was needed was a more proactive approach, aiming at increasing integration but only at the conditions that the Egyptian economy and society could sustain. With their knowledge of complex technicalities of the global economy, the discourse went, local technocrats and businessmen are best placed to allow Egypt to reap the benefits of integration while minimising its negative externalities. On the other hand, there was an increasing awareness within the regime of the need to increase participation away from the 'second stratum' of bureaucrats and party officials that had dominated political life. The new business class was extremely skilful in portraying itself as a much needed injection of civil society, and of a younger generation, within the regime. The presence of Gamal would make sure that it would keep playing by the rules, while providing an increase in the representativeness of the regime and attracting the support of international organisations, donors and investors. And their money.

The power and limits of neoliberalism: just an ideology for the few?

Given the speed with which economic reforms, particularly in the financial sector, proceeded since 2004, it is possible to see how ideas can become a powerful driver of economic and political change even when they are held by a small yet extremely influential group of individuals. This is particularly true in the case of authoritarian regimes, where meaningful decision-making is by definition concentrated in the hands of few people. In this respect, neoliberalism provided a much needed ideological platform that attracted the support of enough people to take control of economic policy-making within the regime. Once this happened, economic reforms and ensuing transformations followed suit, with both intended and unintended consequences.

DOI: 10.1057/9781137395924

At the same time, the reliance on neoclassical economics on the theoretical side and neoliberalism on the policy side allowed a restructuring of the discourse around a set of assumptions that would effectively lock in reforms. Three of these assumptions deserve more specific attention here. Firstly, all Egyptian economic problems were framed under a state vs. market dichotomy. This was the organising principle of the structural adjustment programme back in 1991, bringing with it the corollary that state intervention was the problem and had to be reduced to a minimum so that market forces could play out and determine an efficient outcome. Whereas the second half of the 1990s showed how this view still encountered resistance within some components of the regime, with the rise of the capitalist oligarchy this mindset became one of the guiding principles of economic policy, in some occasions preventing the consideration of alternative solutions. This is for example visible in the reaction to the blatant failure of the new tenancy law in increasing agricultural productivity. In this respect, more of the same neoliberal policies were considered the solution. The rollback of the Nasserist land reform redesigned the boundaries of what was thinkable with respect to agricultural reforms, excluding *a priori* alternative measures that had been successful in countries with similar constraints and at comparable levels of economic development. As Mitchell put it, '[t]he redistribution of agricultural land offered a workable and proven means of creating sustainable rural livelihoods. [...] But in official studies of the obstacles to Egypt's further economic development, the question of additional land reform was simply never raised' (2002: 221).

The dichotomy between state and market came with the inevitable corollary that saw the private sector as inherently more efficient than the public sector in terms of welfare maximisation. This in turn rests on the neoclassical assumption that sees markets as characterised by perfect competition and full availability of information to all actors involved, and further assumes actors as fully rational and able to process all the pieces of information contained in market signals. Within this context, public actors' choices are always necessarily distorted by extra-economic priorities concerning the management and maintenance of power, whereas this does not happen for private actors. Driven exclusively by self-interest, the latter are better placed to achieve welfare-maximising outcomes. Applied to the Egyptian case, this reasoning led to a call for downsizing the public sector, so that private actors would be able to step

DOI: 10.1057/9781137395924

in and create a more efficient economy. A signal of the cognitive lock brought about by these assumptions can be seen in the inability on the part of the regime to think of any industrial policy that would go beyond the reorganisation of state-owned enterprises followed by their privatisation. In the very semantic conflation of SOEs and assets, one can see how the value of public industrial companies was limited to its sale value, thus effectively forsaking any option of a more activist industrial policy, fundamental for the success of most newly developed countries (Chang 2002).

Another key assumption framing the neoliberal discourse, and hence the practice carried out particularly from 2004 on, relates to considering liberalisation – be it of trade, prices or capital movements – as an unquestionably positive thing for the Egyptian economy. Again, the micro-economic foundations of this argument are the same discussed above on the issue of efficiency: in a market characterised by perfect competition and perfect information any form of interference with market forces, for example in the form of barriers or controls, leads at best to suboptimal outcomes. However, if the establishment of market is prioritised, and the flow of goods and services is to be facilitated as much as possible, then exchange appears to take precedence over production (Abdel-Khalek 2001: 42). Once more, this tendency was also reproduced in political language, with the historically separate ministries of industry and trade being merged into the Ministry of Trade (i.e. exchange) and Industry (i.e. production). The very order given to the two components of the ministry were arguably the clearest statement of Rashid's policy mission.

The inherent preference for capital account liberalisation provides an even stronger case in this respect. This is because, as put by Chwieroth (2010: 44–7), theoretical arguments for and against capital freedom are equally powerful, and equally supported by economic theories, and the preference of each economist largely depends on the economic doctrine she subscribes to.[6] Despite this contested theoretical ground, financial sector reform in Egypt was entirely framed under the assumption that the benefits of capital freedom would outweigh its costs.

This was nowhere clearer than in the EU-supported implementation of Basel II regulation for the national banking sector. The Basel II framework was designed by highly developed countries to cope with regulatory problems in their own banking sectors. Yet, when applied to less developed countries the very same regulations might have had a

DOI: 10.1057/9781137395924

damaging impact on the strength and stability of the domestic financial sector. Griffith-Jones identifies five major areas on which the Basel II agreement either neglected to take into account the needs of developing countries or risked to create further problems in their banking systems (2007: 2–3): neglect of key sources of banking sector vulnerabilities typical of developing countries, such as currency mismatches; overall reduction of credit levels; reinforcement of procyclicality of lending, with following increase in volatility; disincentives to lend to small and medium enterprises; competitive advantage for more internationalised banks, which in the case of developing countries usually means foreign banks. Several interviews conducted with CBE officials revealed that only the foreign exchange exposure of domestic banks was considered of some importance in the Egyptian case, possibly because the black currency exchange market, which created so many troubles to the official economy, had disappeared only in the early 2000s.

Other than providing a unifying platform for different groups within the NDP and a way of foreclosing the discussion of different options, neoliberalism effectively became what in the constructivist literature is called a 'policy paradigm', whose main characteristic is that it is 'embedded in the very terminology through which policy-makers communicate about their work, and it is influential precisely because so much of it is taken for granted and unamenable to scrutiny as a whole' (Hall 1993: 279). By shaping the overall economic *problematique*, neoliberalism also started to feed back on the perceptions of the capitalist oligarchy, whose interests came to be perceived as increasingly tied to the further withdrawal of the state from the economy and the increased marketisation of the latter.

Lastly, and arguably most importantly, the translation of neoliberal ideology into policy served extremely well the interests of its main supporters. The way in which the acceleration on the reform path brought a substantial increase in wealth and power for the new capitalist class has already been discussed at length in the previous chapter. The timing in their seize of political power is better captured through reference to the role of ideas in creating new boundaries with respect to what should be thought of as economic policy, and in instilling some biases with respect to the preferred options to be followed within those boundaries. In understanding this relation between material power relations and how the way they are perceived and understood end up reshaping them, it makes sense to refer back to Stuart Hall's remark that '[m]aterial

DOI: 10.1057/9781137395924

conditions are the necessary but not sufficient condition of all historical practice' (1996: 147).

If neoliberalism as an ideology was extremely successful for reorienting economic policy in a direction beneficial to the emerging new business class, it does not necessarily follow that the articulation proposed was equally successful in penetrating common sense in the wider society. Rather, the emphasis on the private sector seizing the opportunities created by state retrenchment, combined with the occupation of the main political positions at both party and cabinet level, appeared to encourage a 'winner-take-all' attitude to both business and politics. The various forms of predatory behaviour displayed by the capitalist oligarchy could not but create resentment both within the regime and in society at large.

As it created deeper divisions within the ruling bloc, the translation of neoliberalism into a practical political project also failed to win much support in most of Egyptian society. Here we finally get to the heart of the matter: if the Nasserist hegemony was limited to begin with, and had been gradually dismantled by both Sadat and Mubarak, the version of neoliberalism proposed by the capitalist oligarchy had clearly failed in providing the discursive and practical basis for hegemony on the national scale. Rather, it worked at best in the form of a 'fractured hegemony', constituting the necessary ideational component for what Gramsci called the 'economic–corporate' moment, which is the phase in which a social class, or fraction thereof, becomes aware of the distinctiveness of its own interests, but it is still unable to articulate a political discourse that is able to transcend them and thus attract the support of different social groups. On the other hand, it proved extremely divisive for the rest of Egyptian society, alienating both important sections of the ruling bloc and most of the middle and lower classes.

Thus, the articulation of neoliberalism with the political argument of regime consolidation on different, and allegedly more sustainable, economic ground allowed the new business class to turn into a predatory capitalist oligarchy controlling the most important economic and political levers in the country. At the same time, it failed to provide a successful discourse that would provide the foundations for some form of restructured hegemony both within the regime and in wider society. Rather, this discourse, and the practices stemming from it, alienated ever wider sections of Egyptian society, belonging both to the state and state-dependent bourgeoisie and to the middle and working classes. As neoliberalism contributed greatly to the fortunes of the new outward-

DOI: 10.1057/9781137395924

oriented business class, it also weakened dramatically the foundations of the regime it was meant to consolidate.

Conclusion

An approach informed by articulation such as the one developed in this work allows us to appreciate the relevance of constructivist insights in studying the penetration of neoliberalism as a new ideological and policy paradigm in Egyptian policy-making. This was particularly visible in the internalisation of specific neoliberal assumptions, ranging from the greater efficiency of the private over the public to the unambiguously positive view of all forms of liberalisation. At the same time, referring to Gramsci and Stuart Hall's annotation that 'everything is within the discursive, but nothing is only discourse or only discursive' (1997: 31) provides a way of relocating the role of ideology within a social context characterised by classes and fractions of classes that are ultimately vying for power.

At the same time, despite this rootedness in material conditions, we have also seen how ideational forces were relatively autonomous, and in reshaping the discourse on economic policy-making in Egypt they also influenced and fed back on social structure. This happened in two different yet largely complementary forms. On the one hand, the affirmation of neoclassical models and neoliberal policies led to a redefinition of the boundaries of economics, what its problems are, the solutions offered and the expected payoff. In this respect, the reorganisation of ideology on the part of organic intellectuals, when successful, turns into policies that have a specific impact on material conditions. In the Egyptian case, we have seen that this impact can be summed up in the accumulation of wealth and power in the hands of a small outward-oriented section of Egyptian capital. Thus, whereas this was perhaps in its origins an instrumental use of ideology for the benefit of its promoters, neoliberal ideas became a causal force of their own, effectively reinforcing and locking in the trends the capitalist oligarchy had wished for. This happened through the identification and definition of some problems as urgent and the neglect of others, through privileging some solutions and overlooking alternatives, and by this eventually reshaping those very material conditions from which they arose, thus to some degree outliving them.

On the other hand, the relatively autonomous impact of neoliberal ideas on the social structure can also be seen in a series of

DOI: 10.1057/9781137395924

unintended – or at least seriously underestimated – consequences. Two of them have received particular attention in this chapter. Firstly, within the ruling bloc, the material impact of the application of neoliberal ideas was a substantial deepening of the division between outward-oriented capitalists on the one hand and crony capitalists and the public sector component on the other hand. From this followed the upset of the delicate balance between the different components supporting the regime. Secondly, with respect to social relations at large, neoliberalism not only produced a phenomenal concentration of wealth and power in the hands of a few, but it also impoverished the middle classes and the poorer strata in society, to be identified in industrial workers, the peasants and the increasing number of urban dwellers relying on the informal labour market.

Thus, we have seen how neoliberalism articulated with a political discourse based on regime consolidation was successful in 'economic-corporate' phase, allowing the new business class to achieve prominence within the ruling bloc, but it failed miserably in providing the basis for a renewed top-down hegemony to be diffused in Egyptian society, as it had happened, even though in a partial and idiosyncratic form, under Nasser. This is not to argue that there must necessarily be a clash between neoliberalism as a policy and cognitive paradigm and the pre-existing corporatist and patron–client arrangements characterising the Egyptian political economy. Indeed, the 'clash of mental models' suggested by Snyder (2007) appears to have been largely dispelled by the economic trajectory taken in post-revolutionary Egypt. The acceptance of the broad contours of the neoliberal economic discourse within a deeply religious and conservative vision of social and political life was one of the centrepieces of the short-lived Muslim Brotherhood-led government. This suggests that other forms of articulation, deriving not from the state but rather from civil society, had developed in parallel to the discourse brought forward by the capitalist oligarchy. Indeed, the very retrenchment of the state provided the social spaces for an increase in grass-roots political and economic activity that was to win the support of vast swathes of the Egyptian population, particularly in the lower social strata. But the rise and fall of neoliberal Islamism, its role in the collapse of the Mubarak regime, and even more in the current state of affairs in post-revolutionary Egypt, is something that is best left to the conclusion of this book.

DOI: 10.1057/9781137395924

Notes

1 One should keep in mind that in Egypt economic nationalism had roots that have been traced back to well before the Free Officers coup, and particularly to the 'Egyptianisation' movement of the 1920s, largely coalescing around the figure of Talaat Harb (Wahba 1994: 37–43; Vitalis 1995: 47–9; Ezzel Arab 2002: 3).

2 Interview with AmCham official, 29 April 2010.

3 Whilst there is certainly not a one-to-one correspondence between neoclassical economics and neoliberal policies, the assumptions of the former significantly foreclose economic policy options, and thus constitute a necessary – though in itself not sufficient – precondition for the promotion of neoliberal policies. For a more detailed outline of the relation between neoclassical economic theory and neoliberalism with respect to capital account liberalisation, see Chwieroth 2010: 61–104.

4 More specifically, for Noland and Pack the lessons to be drawn by Middle Eastern countries from the East Asian miracle are the following: the importance of macroeconomic stability, low inflation and competitive exchange rates, high rates of accumulation of both human and fiscal capital, education, micro-economic and institutional quality (2005: 18–22).

5 This assurance was not universally perceived or well received, as witnessed by the controversies, particularly in the army, regarding the increasing concentration of power in the hands of Gamal Mubarak and his supporters. These aspects will be discussed in greater depth in the next chapter.

6 Incidentally, this was also confirmed in the late 1990s by an independent evaluation carried out by the IMF surveillance system, which argued that within the Fund the opposition to capital controls 'was based more on ideology than on a careful consideration of the evidence and the policy alternatives' (IMF 1999: 39).

DOI: 10.1057/9781137395924

5

From Hubris to Debris: Global Crisis and the End of the Mubarak Regime

Abstract: *By recasting the discussion in broader historical and geographical terms, this chapter advances two arguments. Firstly, while neoliberal reforms under Mubarak certainly accelerated this process, a gradual unravelling of hegemony on the national scale was already taking place at least since the 1970s. Secondly, both the global food crisis and the global financial crisis are better seen as triggers which interacted with the socio-economic devastations produced by two decades of reform. This turned a latent hegemonic crisis into an actual one, thus making the 2011 revolution possible.*

Keywords: Egyptian revolution; hegemonic crisis, global food crisis; global financial crisis; Mubarak's fall

Roccu, Roberto. *The Political Economy of the Egyptian Revolution: Mubarak, Economic Reforms and Failed Hegemony*. Basingstoke: Palgrave Macmillan, 2014. DOI: 10.1057/9781137395924.

DOI: 10.1057/9781137395924

It is now time to pull threads together, in order to assess to which degree each of the three dimensions discussed in the previous chapters impacted on the constitution of hegemony on the national scale in Egypt. As Ayubi aptly noted (1995: 33–4), while semantically broader and theoretically deeper, hegemony is undoubtedly correlated to legitimacy, in that each hegemonic crisis presents itself also as a legitimacy crisis, and each successful hegemony allows specific classes, or fractions thereof, to rule without constantly questioning their legitimacy for doing so. Given that it is now undoubted that the lost legitimacy of the Mubarak regime features heavily among the reasons for the protests leading to its overthrow, one would expect hegemony on the national scale to have been eroded significantly in the years or in the decades preceding the 2011 revolution. Integrating the effects of articulation on the international–national, economic–political, material–ideational dimensions allows us to show the failure of neoliberalism in finding a solution to the hegemonic crisis of the Mubarak regime. Indeed, the first section of this chapter suggests that the reforms implemented accelerated an already incipient process of unravelling of the Nasserist hegemony.

If this point is established, it is then necessary to look at how exogenous factors, identified more specifically in the global food crisis of 2007 and the global financial crisis of 2008, impacted the prospects of the capitalist oligarchy of bolstering the same political regime through a shift towards a different accumulation regime. More specifically, the second section argues that, while neither of the two global crises had a strong impact on the Egyptian political economy, they contributed in two main ways in making the latent legitimacy crisis an apparent one. On the one hand, they showed the increasing inability on the part of the state to function as a backstop against exogenous shocks once integration in the global economy had taken place. On the other hand, it further showed the polarising effects of neoliberal reforms, as once aggregate indicators started to worsen it became apparent that some social strata were still shielded from the crisis, and on some occasions might actually benefit from it, whereas increasing swathes of the Egyptian population were exposed only to the costs of integration in the global economy. This was arguably the highest social cost of differential integration. In the instantiation carried out by the capitalist oligarchy, the neoliberal project failed to become hegemonic in any meaningful sense, and indeed opened up the way for an alliance of social forces opposed to the regime which – however temporary – managed to overthrow the president, and

DOI: 10.1057/9781137395924

eventually to scapegoat the most visible elements of the new business class who had pushed so hard for a thorough neoliberalisation of the national economy.

Hegemony unravelling: a longer-term perspective (1952–2010)

In order to integrate the impact of neoliberal reforms on hegemony in Egypt with pre-existing trends it might be helpful to cast the evolution on the three dimensions discussed in the previous chapters with a brief recollection of how state hegemony was constructed, reproduced and to some degree transformed already under Nasser and Sadat. In other words, casting a look backwards to the six decades of Egypt as an independent republic might help us put into a broader perspective the benefits and damages produced by neoliberalism in the form it penetrated the Egyptian political economy.

Under Nasser, Egypt was able to develop a positional rent firstly by sitting on the fence in the confrontation between superpowers, getting in this way loans and grants from both sides, and then by being extremely proactive in the creation of the Non-Aligned Movement. These were the times of Keynesianism as the dominant discourse in international economic policy, with strong capital controls containing the thrust of global capital accumulation, thus allowing for forms of articulation where the autonomy of the national scale was much less limited. Starting from these conditions, the articulation of the economic and the political led to the emergence of a state capitalist accumulation regime, committed to both development and equality, while at the same time saw the gradual elimination of most of the pre-existing elites, the establishment of a populist social pact aimed at repressing class conflict, and the consolidation of an authoritarian regime dominated by the army. On the material–ideational dimension, Nasser's regime relied on a strong tradition of economic nationalism, compounded in the first decade by Pan-Arab ambitions. All of this was underpinned by a ruling bloc including the ever-expanding public sector, and allegedly also industrial workers and peasants, away from the 'half–per-cent' society of colonial Egypt. This suggests that Nasser was able to establish a distinctly Egyptian form of hegemony that had some degree of effectiveness. It was certainly not an 'integral' hegemony, as

DOI: 10.1057/9781137395924

demonstrated by extremely limited political participation as well as by the ruthless repression of opposition groups, and particularly of the Muslim Brotherhood.[1] Yet, the regime was not predominantly based on coercion, as it was able to provide both material and symbolic benefits to most strata of society, with the exclusion of the expropriated land-owning elites and *comprador* bourgeoisie who had been successfully cast in the public discourse as servants of imperialist forces and thus obstacles to Egypt's rise.

The Six-Day war brought this phase to an abrupt end, as witnessed by the 30 March Programme in 1968, which constitutes a first relaxation of the state's grip on the national economy (Bush 1999: 15). Under Sadat, even if the accumulation regime remained an *étatist* one, it was already possible to detect some significant transformations on each of the three dimensions analysed. The most glaring one was obviously related to interscalar articulation, with the peace treaty with Israel and the realign-ment with the West significantly changing the structure of opportunities and constraints facing the Egyptian government. The sudden increase in external assistance particularly coming from the US, together with larger private capital flows allowed by *infitah*, were instrumental in bringing about a mass consumer society, but at the same time failed to win the support of the masses, particularly on the hugely controversial issue of Arab–Israeli relations. On the other hand, the rise of neoliberalism on the international scale started to put the Egyptian accumulation regime under severe pressure. Yet, the vital strategic importance of Egypt in the Middle East peace process was used to good effect to resist pressures towards more thoroughgoing economic reform. On the articulation of economic and political factors, *infitah* started a process of economic and political liberalisation that, while significantly weakened on both dimen-sions already a few years after its launch, spurred social changes that in turn produced a reorganisation of power within the ruling bloc and in society as a whole. The most relevant transformation was arguably the creation of the *infitah* bourgeoisie, which as already mentioned became a junior partner of the army in the ruling bloc. Lastly, with respect to the interaction of material and ideational factors, after the 1979 elections the populist discourse inherited from Nasserism was replaced by politi-cal demobilisation, which opened the way to the resurgence of Islamist groups. In his first decade in power, Mubarak continued along this route. The economic liberalism underpinning *infitah* was largely neutralised by the *dirigist* preferences of the still dominant public sector. These

DOI: 10.1057/9781137395924

transformations also had an impact on the constitution of hegemony, particularly as material benefits in the form of welfare programmes started to be gradually withdrawn and were only partially replaced by increased mass consumption, which dramatically increased the import bill thus contributing to the cyclical fiscal problems of the state. Thus, hegemony on the national scale had already started to decline, and was somehow 'fractured', holding together the ruling bloc through the asymmetrical alliance between the army and the *infitah* class, but starting to lose its grip on the rest of society.

This broader historical perspective sheds a different light on the material presented in the previous chapters, suggesting that a gradual unravelling of hegemony on the national scale was already taking place, and that this trend was considerably accelerated by the implementation of neoliberal reforms. Transformations produced by articulations on each of the three dimensions supports this view. Firstly, on the spatial dimension, the affirmation of neoliberalism on the international scale spurred a process of economic restructuring by which the accumulation regime was gradually transformed in the direction promoted by globalising capital and its main international supporters, be they IFIs, donors or investors. At the same time, this reliance of an accumulation regime increasingly prevalent on the international scale was not adequately articulated with a national hegemonic project. This element paradoxically emerged in an ever clearer form once economic reforms started to be driven by Egyptian policy-makers, largely in the name of the new business class. When discussing hegemony in Chapter 1, it was emphasised that despite its inescapable links to processes of global capital accumulation, hegemony must have a social basis on the national scale in order to work. On this aspect it would appear that the rising capitalist oligarchy failed miserably in elaborating this link between an accumulation regime increasingly linked to global capital and a support base larger than their own numbers for such a socio-economic shift. Rather, the neoliberal project was perceived as being carried out with the only aim of favouring the narrow interests of a social group, and a small one for that matter.

Secondly, the articulation of the economic and the political shows how neoliberal reforms, by promoting and reinforcing the rise of a capitalist oligarchy at the expense of both the other components of the ruling bloc and the rest of the population, produced a reorganisation of power whose stability was much more apparent than real. If the success of a

DOI: 10.1057/9781137395924

hegemonic project is dependent on its ability to relate to an existing or prospective accumulation regime, and the social relations sustaining it, then the rising capitalist elite fell well short of fostering this link, relying more on crony and predatory practices than on its potential leadership of a new hegemonic project.

Thirdly, with respect to the articulation of material and ideational factors, the rise of neoliberalism as an economic ideology has been discussed with reference to its success in the academic, policy-making and business community. However, beyond these areas increasingly influenced by the power of the capitalist oligarchy, neoliberalism proved divisive both in the ruling bloc and in the wider society. In the former, this happened mostly because neoliberalism pitted the public and private sector components one against the other, thus creating a low-intensity conflict that jeopardised the precarious balance of social forces ensuring regime stability. In the latter, the divisiveness of neoliberalism was rooted in its material consequences, as it brought sizeable benefits to a small stratum while impoverishing the rest of the population. Recalling Sassoon's definition of hegemony as exchange mentioned in Chapter 1, we should keep in mind that these exchanges are not exclusively discursive, but also entail the delivery (or promise) of real (or prospective) improvements to the life of those involved, be they different fractions of the ruling bloc or subaltern groups. Once refined and systematically organised by organic intellectuals, political practice increasingly became permeated by neoliberal ideology. Here the devastating impact of these new policies on the Egyptian social fabric contributed in a major way to exposing fractures between the capitalist oligarchy and the rest of Egyptian society. This was a further element suggesting how the sources of hegemony in Egypt, already weakened by *infitah*, had gradually been drained by neoliberal reforms.

Transformations on the dimensions evaluated by this work suggest that national hegemony in Egypt experienced a substantial erosion since the 1980s, which accelerated dramatically since the adoption of stabilisation and adjustment measures. If under Nasser hegemony was not 'integral', it was to some degree effective, especially in the wake of the Suez crisis. *Infitah* produced a fracturing of the system, still hegemonic in the face of the ruling bloc, but increasingly less so towards the rest of the population. It is only with neoliberal reforms, though, that hegemony on the national scale failed, providing one of the premises for the sustained protests leading to the fall of Mubarak.

DOI: 10.1057/9781137395924

Crises at home and abroad: interscalar articulation and the fall of Mubarak

Focusing eminently on the transformations of hegemony on the national scale, this work has somehow bracketed out any potential change occurring on the international scale. This was admissible when discussing the economic reforms undertaken by the Egyptian economy under the sponsorship or informal support of international organisations, donors and investors, as for most of the 1990s and 2000s neoliberal globalisation appeared to be firmly dominant, and arguably on the ascendancy, drawing into its orbit ever larger portions of the global economy. However, the financial crisis of 2007/08 constitutes too big of a shock to be ignored altogether, and the same goes for the global food crisis, as it led to a phenomenal increase in the price of wheat, a staple for most Egyptians.

Other than clarifying the context within which the Egyptian revolution took place, the focus on the crisis of the neoliberal model permits to evaluate two corollaries of what has been discussed so far, thus deepening our understanding of the socio-economic background of the Egyptian revolution. On the one hand, discussing the interscalar articulation of hegemonies and crises allows us to assess under which conditions the decisions of relevant actors on the national scale to rely on an accumulation regime prevalent internationally might work or not, and why. On the other hand, it complements the findings emerged from the previous chapters and helps us moving towards an account of what has happened in Egypt since the January 2011 revolution. More specifically, while the hybrid forms of neoliberalism developed in Egypt effectively accelerated hegemonic failure on the national scale, the crisis of neoliberalism on the international scale produced a further exacerbation of conditions within Egypt, contributing significantly to turning a latent hegemonic crisis into an actual one, and one that is still ongoing, given the instability that has characterised Egypt since the fall of Mubarak.

If one goes back to the late 1980s, the decision on the part of Egyptian policy-makers to shift away from *étatism* and rely more heavily on the accumulation regime increasingly prevalent on the international scale was arguably the only way to go. While defusing pressures coming from international actors, and indeed pleasing some of them to the point of debt cancellation, economic liberalisation could have also brought benefits in terms of economic performance, and by this might have increased regime legitimacy both at home and abroad. The improvements displayed

DOI: 10.1057/9781137395924

by Egypt with respect to its macroeconomic indicators appeared to corroborate this argument. In the peak years of the two waves of reforms, respectively in 1997 and 2008, Egyptian aggregate indicators might have been confused with those of the BRIC (Brazil, Russia, India, China) countries: the economy was growing at a sustained rate (5.5 in 1997, 7.2 in 2008), budget deficit was under control (1.6 in 1997, 6.6 in 2008), large capital inflows seemed to provide the preconditions for successful long-term development. Through increased integration in an expanding global economy, the shift towards a neoliberal accumulation regime appeared to be working well for Egypt.

Despite these promising aggregate outcomes, the highly unequal distribution of benefits and costs stemming from the neoliberal turn meant that a new regime that was successful in its main task – that is, sheer capital accumulation – was actually impoverishing most of the Egyptian population. There were two different elements at play here. On the one hand, even when successful in aggregate terms and thus allowing some developing countries to reduce the gap with developed countries, neoliberal policies have usually had a strong disequalising effect within countries. Egypt was not an exception in this respect. On the other hand, the articulation of neoliberalism with pre-existing corporatist, crony and at times outright corrupt practices meant the benefits deriving from these reforms would almost never exit the regime circuit, and also within such circuit they were more often than not captured by the fraction of the private sector best connected with international capital. Rather than from adopting the neoliberal template *per se*, a large part of the problem for the Egyptian regime derived exactly from this predatory attitude on the part of the rising component of the ruling bloc. It has been discussed how this 'winner-take-all' tendency was also displayed in the political arena. It was apparent that the emerging capitalist oligarchy was not planning, at least in the short run, to give up part of its immediate interests in order to accommodate some of the material and symbolic demands of other social forces, something which would have improved the chances of stabilising the political regime in the long run. In other words, the only social group with the potential of becoming hegemonic either had no interest in constructing a new hegemony on the national scale, or was planning to move in this direction in a second phase, when its prominent position within the ruling bloc would have become unassailable.

The global food crisis in 2007 and the collapse of Lehman Brothers in the following year, with all the financial turmoil that ensued, meant

DOI: 10.1057/9781137395924

that no long-run hopes and calculations would apply anymore. On the former, some scholars went as far as claiming that rising food prices were the single most important explanatory factor of the Arab uprisings (Lagi, Bertrand and Bar-Yam 2011). This argument is certainly exaggerated in the specific Egyptian case. At the same time, as *'eish* (bread) was one of the main slogans echoing in the Egyptian squares and streets flooded with protesters, one might be tempted to look back and see whether increasing food prices might have had at least an indirect role. This is yet another perfect example of the devastations that might occur when unfettered economic integration on neoliberal terms is combined with the survival of inefficient forms of state intervention, producing yet another instance of differential integration. More specifically, the slow yet steady devaluation of the pound since it was allowed to float translated into a similarly steady increase in the price of both food and consumer products, which was obviously felt much more by the working classes. Because of the spike in international prices and the ongoing devaluation of the pound, the import bill for wheat became increasingly onerous both for government and private companies. If one is interested in going even deeper, the shift towards focusing agricultural production in other sectors considered more remunerative such as livestock feed was due to trade liberalisation combined with removal of subsidised inputs in the sector. As a consequence, less and less cereals and legumes were produced, and given the very low demand elasticity of wheat, imports had to grow by a corresponding amount (Bush 2003), thus exposing the Egyptian economy even more to exogenous shocks such as the one that inevitably materialised in 2007. This constellation of negative factors deriving from global integration on neoliberal terms was compounded by the functioning of wheat subsidies, which constituted an incentive for distributors to sell flour to private rather than to state-owned bakeries. This led to a shortage of bread in public bakeries, with the price of bread becoming unaffordable in private bakeries. As Cook put it (2012: 178), '[t]he results are predictable: enough bread, but in the wrong places at the wrong prices, producing long lines at state-owned bakeries, which, without ample flour, were unable to meet demand, pushing prices even higher at nongovernment bakeries'.

Similarly, the global financial crisis did not have a strong direct impact on the Egyptian economy. Indeed, it is fair to say that the dominance of the banking sector, its limited internationalisation, together with the relative lack of sophisticated financial instruments in private capital

DOI: 10.1057/9781137395924

markets, successfully acted as shields against a local financial crisis. Importantly, all of these elements, together with the moderately positive reaction of macroeconomic indicators and the delay with which the crisis hit Egypt are signals of its still partial incorporation in the global political economy, thus suggesting that the process of integration was still far from complete (Talani forthcoming). However, the credit crunch and the effective freezing of global investments inevitably led to the collapse of FDI inflows, one of the instruments on which Mohieldin had focused the most, to the point of being mocked as the 'minister of foreign invest-ment', rather than investment *tout court*, by his opponents.

These two examples portray rather clearly the dire straits in which the state found itself once the shockwaves of both global crises began to be felt on the Egyptian shores. On the one hand, the increasing reliance on private capital flows combined with a less activist state in stimulating economic activity or directly engaging in production dragged the econ-omy back into a phase of low economic growth, which would clearly not suffice to keep the middle and lower classes afloat given the uneven dis-tribution of such growth. On the other hand, the traditional instruments to tame fluctuations in international prices of key goods proved to be entirely counterproductive in an era of ever more integrated global mar-kets, as it happened in the case of wheat, where the divergence between market and subsidised flour price constituted too strong an incentive for poorly controlled distributors who could not but exploit the chance of making quick profits out of the price differential.

This weakening of the regime capacity to face the negative spill-over effects from the global food and financial crises was the first alarm bell for the capitalist oligarchy. The second came during the summer of 2010, when the carefully constructed strategy of gradually raising the political profile of Gamal Mubarak as part of his grooming for succeeding his father was ground to a sudden halt. An allegedly spontaneous grass-roots campaign was launched by some of Gamal's supporters calling for him to run as presidential candidate in the elections that should have been held in 2011. The campaign turned out to be a total disaster, encounter-ing strong resistance both within the NDP and mostly importantly on a popular level.[2] This single event epitomises better than any other how the capitalist oligarchy had failed even in creating its own support base and/or clientele that would support its political rise at the ballot box. The dimension of this disconnect is ever more apparent if one thinks at the praise that many of the members of the neoliberal wing received from

DOI: 10.1057/9781137395924

IFIs, donors and investors. When appointed to the position of managing director of the World Bank group in September 2010, Mohieldin was praised by the then president of the Bank Robert Zoellick as a 'tireless reformer' and '[a]n outstanding young leader' (World Bank 2010c). Yet, even his domestic admirers would have no problems in admitting that he was arguably the least popular minister until in charge. More generally, whereas the man tipped as 'the best change for Egyptian democracy' (Masoud 2010), and the businessmen and technocrats around him won much support within IFIs and among foreign ministries in the developed world, they had failed miserably in winning any form of support among their own fellow citizens.

The third and most important element suggesting that bad times were imminent for the new business class came from the lower classes, and more specifically from the embryonic alliance that started to take place between two sections of protesters that until then the regime had been able to keep separate. On the one hand, the run-up to the 2005 presidential elections saw the emergence of a movement – Kefaya – demanding an end to the emergency law enacted after the killing of Sadat in 1981 and to all laws restricting freedom. Three years later property-tax collectors succeeded in creating trade unions independent from the regime. On the other hand, as already mentioned in Chapter 3, since 2007 there had been a mounting wave of protest in the industrial workplace, particularly in the spinning and weaving factories of the Delta. Whereas historically the strategy of divide-and-rule on the part of the regime had been successful in isolating and containing protests, this time the mobilisation of the urban poor worked as a bridge, both social and geographical, between industrial workers and the urban middle class (Roccu 2013).

If the social consequences of neoliberal reforms on the national scale were a necessary but insufficient cause for the Egyptian revolution to occur, then the indirect impact of the global crisis of neoliberalism contributed by significantly worsening those very socio-economic conditions in which an alliance, however limited and contingent, between working and middle classes had become possible. The inability of the capitalist oligarchy to bring the other main component of the ruling bloc decidedly on their side allowed the army to see the 25 January protests as a chance to reassert their prominence within the regime and in society. Under these starting conditions, the decision on the part of Tantawi to ask Mubarak Sr. to go and the resolution with which the Supreme Council of the Armed Forces pursued the members of the new business

DOI: 10.1057/9781137395924

elite close to Gamal Mubarak would only seem the best way of bending, once more, genuine popular protests to the army's interests. However, this reassertion of dominance was to prove soon more contested than the army itself might have anticipated.

Conclusion

The undoubted *hubris* characterising the rise of the new business class is to be better understood as another signal of their inability to move beyond the economic–corporate moment. Indeed, their resort to predatory behaviours while attempting to articulate a project arguably hegemonic on the international scale had devastating consequences in two respects. On the one hand, there was some attention to intra-regime fixes, particularly with efforts at appeasing the army with side-benefits in the wake of reforms, but these did not prove enough to avoid being seen as a threat to the historically predominant position of the army within the ruling bloc. On the other hand, the inability to move beyond the economic–corporate moment became also the inability to develop a wider hegemonic project, which would promise and to some degree realise a wider distribution of the benefits of economic restructuring. The consequence of this was increasing resentment on the part of impoverished middle and lower classes.

This increasing discontent with the direction taken by the Egyptian political economy both within the regime and in wider society is partly related to the very nature of neoliberalism, which has produced a more skewed distribution of income across the board where it has been implemented. At the same time, this has not prevented neoliberal ideas to become dominant and increasingly accepted by significant sections of subaltern classes in many of these countries (Harvey 2005). In the Egyptian case, increased inequality was combined with the forms of articulations discussed in the previous three chapters, which effectively prevented almost all Egyptians outside of the ruling bloc to enjoy any of the benefits from the years of high growth.

The mediated impact of both the global food and global financial crises instead showed how even the costs of economic reforms had been distributed unevenly, with the impoverished middle classes being doubly exposed to the negative shocks. Firstly, because of the increasingly skewed distribution of benefits the working classes and most sections of

DOI: 10.1057/9781137395924

the middle classes found themselves with less means to face an adverse economic conjuncture. Secondly, the differential integration brought about by neoliberal policies along the lines of privatisation and liberalisation combined with the persistence of inefficient *étatist* instruments created an incentive structure discouraging private sector provision of goods and services to the lower classes. This was particularly visible in the abovementioned bread crisis.

It was then hardly surprising that the capitalist oligarchy would serve as a convenient scapegoat, although – to be clear – one with eminent responsibilities for the disastrous socio-economic conditions Egypt was in. At that time, as in the more recent intervention to oust Morsi, there was a contingent convergence of interests between protesters and the army, which appeared committed to democratic transition. The criticism that SCAF attracted from most quarters during the first transitional phase, and their decision to at least partially give in to popular pressures suggested that 'the power of the people is greater than the people in power', to cite Wael Ghonim (2012). However, the rise and fall of the capitalist oligarchy appears to have been followed by the even faster rise and fall of the Muslim Brotherhood. In the meanwhile, the army has taken control again. Is this the end of the Egyptian revolution?

Notes

1   Incidentally, Nasser's full-on war against the Muslim Brotherhood is believed to have played a key role in the radicalisation of the movement, as it forced many members of the groups to flee the country towards Saudi Arabia, and there come in contact with Wahhabism, which clearly influenced the ideological development of the Brotherhood and of its actions in Egypt once its members were allowed to return to the country under Sadat.

2   'Gamal Mubarak nomination campaign a "fiasco", says Kefaya leader', *Daily News Egypt*, 26 July 2010.

DOI: 10.1057/9781137395924

Conclusion: Gramsci, Failed Hegemony and the Fall of Mubarak

Abstract: *The conclusion attempts to systematically outline the method of articulation and its links to the key Gramscian concept of hegemony. It then discusses how this approach provides a deeper yet more nuanced understanding of the causes of the Egyptian revolution. More specifically, neoliberal reforms are to be seen as a necessary, but by no means sufficient, condition for the popular uprisings leading to the fall of Mubarak to occur.*

Keywords: Gramsci; method of articulation; Egyptian revolution; fall of Mubarak

Roccu, Roberto. *The Political Economy of the Egyptian Revolution: Mubarak, Economic Reforms and Failed Hegemony*. Basingstoke: Palgrave Macmillan, 2014. DOI: 10.1057/9781137395924.

This conclusion gives us the chance for a brief recollection of the theoretical and empirical contributions of this work. The first section sketches a more systematic understanding of the method of articulation, and how this is linked to the key Gramscian concept of hegemony. The second section discusses how this method has been deployed towards the study of the political economy of reforms under Mubarak. It shows how the reforms carried out since the late 1980s transformed the Egyptian economy in a neoliberal direction, with the rise of a new business class creating discontent in the army, while on the other hand inequality was rampant in wider society. Unsurprisingly these developments eroded any remnants of hegemony, and thus legitimacy, enjoyed by the Mubarak regime. In other words, neoliberal reforms in the way they were carried out in Egypt were a necessary, yet by no means sufficient, condition for the Egyptian revolution to occur.

Back to Gramsci: the method of articulation in brief

Whereas most neo-Gramscian approaches aimed at establishing a critical theory of IR, the theoretical aim of this study was considerably less ambitious. More than developing an alternative *theory*, the intention here was to explore how Gramsci can provide a sound starting point for establishing an alternative *method* for studying changes and continuities in the global political economy. Following Gramsci's suggestion, rather than focusing on select concepts that might provide the grounding for a theory, this work has looked for the *leitmotiv* of his thinking and tried to trace down its methodological basis.

The *leitmotiv* of Gramsci's thinking was identified in the 'philosophy of praxis', which in its very name contains a manifesto for the method of articulation, as it implies the coexistence and mutual constitution of theory and practice. As it allows ideas to feed back on material conditions and eventually influence their evolution, the philosophy of praxis already contains what is considered the main innovation brought by Gramsci to twentieth-century Marxism: the transformation of the increasingly rigid and mechanistic base-superstructure metaphor into a more flexible relation where superstructural developments also produce transformations at the structural level. Thus, Gramsci conceives the relation between structure and superstructure as an open-ended and never-ending interaction whose results are by definition provisional,

DOI: 10.1057/9781137395924

in a dialectic where the structure sets the boundaries for action which to an extent are constantly redrawn by actions themselves on the level of superstructure. This interactive understanding is best embodied in the concept of 'historical bloc', with the former term referring to the contingent conditions underlying any given relation between structure and superstructure, and the latter identifying the inescapable relation between the realm of production and the realm of state and civil society relations.

This work has suggested that a disaggregation of the different instances of the structure–superstructure relation is most helpful when adopting the method of articulation to study the global political economy. Such choice dispels even more forcefully the risks of economic determinism. This is done by showing how the globalising tendencies of capital accumulation are fragmented, refracted and at times also transformed on three different dimensions, entailing the interaction of respectively: the international and the national, the economic and the political, the material and the ideational. In this respect, the main contribution of the method of articulation to critical IPE lies in the chance of retaining the structural grounding by acknowledging the shaping power held by social relations of production, while at the same time suggesting in which form their mediation on the realm of superstructures leads to a fragmentation and transformation of the logic of capital accumulation. In other words, the method of articulation allows us to bring respectively the national, the political, the ideational back in – to use a fashionable expression – eschewing globalist, economistic and vulgar materialist tendencies.

The potential of this approach has been illustrated with reference to the political economy of reforms in Egypt in the 1990s and 2000s, with an eye to how transformations on these three dimensions have influenced the constitution, reproduction and transformation of hegemony, the most commonly used Gramscian concept. Because of relatively limited ways of researching the role of private actors in the Egyptian economy and the historically predominant position of the state in the economy and society in the whole Middle East, this research has mostly focused on the state and its institutions, paying particular attention at the different components striving for relevance and prominence within the regime. However, the focus on the state in the specific Egyptian case need not imply the impossibility of extending the method of articulation to the study of other instances of the national, the political and the ideational.

DOI: 10.1057/9781137395924

In sum, whereas relatively coherent in its abstract–theoretical form, once translated in concrete–complex terms (Jessop 1982), and thus once articulated with territoriality, politics and ideas, the logic of capital accumulation in the age of neoliberal globalisation becomes much more fragmented and varied than is often assumed in critical IPE. Indeed, the forms of hybridisation of neoliberalism could have been enriched by the study of other forms of the political, the national and the ideational that were not treated in this work. For example, the informal one-party system dominated by the NDP prevented an appreciation of the role that political partisanship might have on the articulation of economic and political factors. This is something that now could be explored by referring more systematically to how the Muslim Brotherhood attempted to articulate similar economic imperatives with rather different social and political goals. Similarly, the focus on IFIs in the study of interscalar articulation translated into a relative neglect of the role of both private capital and money coming from non-Western countries in influencing the options that actors on the national scale were faced with. For instance, the role played by aid and loans provided by the regional powers such as Saudi Arabia and Qatar is an issue that would deserve further investigation. Lastly, the impact of the structure could be further mediated by articulation among different discourses, which have been overlooked to focus exclusively on the economic policy discourse. In the Egyptian case, this might have meant analysing how neoliberalism interacted with various Islamist discourses and to what effect. Yet, already in the form delineated here, the method of articulation provides the tools to venture beyond the two decades of neoliberal reforms and into the political economy of the revolution and everything that followed the fall of Mubarak.

Neoliberal Egypt as failed hegemony: key findings

Four main findings have emerged from adopting the method of articulation in the study of the political economy of reforms in Egypt in the 1990s and 2000s. Firstly, the Egyptian economy changed significantly in a neoliberal direction. The fiscal crisis of the late 1980s provided a must-take opportunity for IFIs to push the set of reforms that since the beginning of the decade had increasingly been adopted in several developing countries, with the aim of transforming them into open export-oriented

DOI: 10.1057/9781137395924

economies. Despite considerable disagreements, both macroeconomic stabilisation and structural adjustment measures were carried out in Egypt, initiating a shift from an *étatist* towards a neoliberal accumulation regime. Relying on the definition of neoliberalisation provided by Harvey, we have seen that what happened in Egypt amounts to such a process. The late 1980s crisis was managed and manipulated by the regime in order to open up the economic system, through a combination of liberalisations and privatisations that provided the conditions for the rise of a capitalist oligarchy. At the same time, slow but steady reforms in the tax code and a much greater reliance on the financial sector produced a redistribution of wealth in favour of large capital owners leading to a further increase in inequality. Whereas these trends might have been partially obscured by the persistence of previous patterns, particularly with reference to the continued dominance of informal networks over formal frameworks, it is difficult to maintain that the penetration of neoliberalism in the Egyptian economy was not a game-changing event.

Secondly, the spatial sources of neoliberalism evolved over time, with the articulation of international and national scale leading to a process of economic restructuring that was arguably pushed down the throat of the Egyptian government in its first phases. However, already during the early 1990s the regime showed great ability with respect to delaying, implementing only partially and sometimes also resisting specific measures. This behaviour seems to suggest a role for the state well beyond that of 'transmission belt' attributed to it by Cox and Robinson. Rather, as the most relevant actor on the nodal scale, the state articulated pressures towards economic reforms in a neoliberal direction with its imperative of maintaining, and whenever possible strengthen, the stability of the political regime. The ability on the part of domestic policy-makers to influence the policies adopted increased significantly as around 2003/04 the push for reforms shifted from IFIs to local outward-oriented businessmen and technocrats who managed to gain political relevance within the regime. This ability of Egyptian policy-makers to influence the timing, sequencing and content of reforms constitutes the first form of hybridisation of the neoliberal template as concretely applied in Egypt.

Thirdly, the second form of hybridisation is provided by the articulation between economic and political factors, which made sure that the form of neoliberalism emerging in Egypt differed considerably from the versions seen in most other countries. The common points with neoliberalism as we came to know it in Western Europe and the Americas

DOI: 10.1057/9781137395924

included an economy mostly owned by private actors, economic policies shaped by neoclassical economic theory, and the increased concentration of wealth and power in the hands of a small minority. However, the Egyptian way to neoliberalism was characterised by peculiarities deriving from the articulation between a shifting accumulation regime and the existing political regime, and the relations of force embedded therein. In particular, we discussed how on the institutional level one can see the increased relevance of privatisations and liberalisations, but also the political rise of the new business class emerged from these very reforms and of select technocrats unified by a neoliberal outlook. Informal mechanisms, on the other hand, show the capture of most privatised companies and liberalised markets by members of the ruling bloc, often belonging to either the *infitah* bourgeoisie or the new business class, but occasionally also the army, as well as the construction of business alliances aimed at raising informal barriers to entry in the most profitable sectors. This shows an attempt to reconstruct authoritarian rule on different economic foundations, with a corresponding redistribution of power within the ruling bloc which gradually saw the new business class turn into a capitalist oligarchy. Despite the attempts to articulate new policies with the pre-existing corporatist and crony arrangements, the form of neoliberal authoritarianism that emerged appeared extremely fragile from the outset, because of the fractures it created and nurtured both within the regime and between the regime and society.

Lastly, if over time neoliberal policies came to be promoted and implemented from the inside, the study of the articulation of material and ideational forces suggests that economic ideas played a major role in this internalisation of neoliberalism. The study of the two main economic think-tanks in Egypt shows their fundamental role in the emergence within the capitalist elite of neoliberalism as a new economic paradigm. This rise of neoliberalism as an ideology had far-reaching consequences on material conditions too. On the one hand, neoliberalism provided new cognitive boundaries to understand what is to be considered as 'economic', relying on the neoclassical synthesis to draw the line between 'the economy' and other social activities which the economists, and economic policy-makers, should not be concerned with. On the other hand, it also provided cognitive biases that identified and framed problems arising in the economic sphere and suggested policy solutions to them. This was seen for example with respect to the often unreflexive preference for private over public sector and for capital account liberalisation.

DOI: 10.1057/9781137395924

The material consequences of these ideas became visible once neoliberal policies were implemented, as they further tilted the distribution of benefits from reforms in favour of the very social group that had been committed to the policy shift to begin with. At the same time, neoliberalism failed to provide an ideological platform around which social groups other than large private capital could coalesce, thus preventing the emergence of an alternative hegemonic discourse from within the regime.

Linking these findings back to Mohieldin's comment at the start of the book, it is possible to say that this time was different because neoliberalism had become a powerful force in the Egyptian political economy. However, the penetration of neoliberalism was mediated by articulation on different levels. This led to the emergence of a neoliberal authoritarian regime as a result of a process of economic restructuring in which the imperatives of global capital accumulation were related to the objective of maintaining authoritarian rule. This time was different because the socio-economic transformations produced by these reforms were over time reinforced by the political rise of the capitalist oligarchy, disgruntling the army which for the first time in the history of republican Egypt saw its own primacy seriously challenged. This time was different because the rise of the capitalist oligarchy meant that their neoliberal ideas became even more widely implemented, further exacerbating the increasing inequalities in Egyptian society. This time was different because neoliberal reforms, partly because of their very nature and partly because of the differential way in which they integrated Egypt in the global economy, created a constellation of social forces that would prove lethal for the Mubarak regime.

DOI: 10.1057/9781137395924

Postscript: Back to Square One? Considerations on Egypt's Uncertain Future

Roccu, Roberto. *The Political Economy of the Egyptian Revolution: Mubarak, Economic Reforms and Failed Hegemony.* Basingstoke: Palgrave Macmillan, 2014.
DOI: 10.1057/9781137395924.

▶

DOI: 10.1057/9781137395924

To make a long story short, the fall of Mubarak could not have happened as it did without the economic reforms of the 1990s and 2000s, informed by neoliberalism and articulated with pre-existing forms of social relations. This does not mean that the socio-economic transformations provoked by these reforms were in themselves both a necessary and a sufficient condition for the 2011 revolution to occur. However, even though counterfactuals are always a risky business, a constellation of social forces such as the one that emerged in the run-up to the revolution would have probably never existed without the devastating social consequences produced by neoliberal reforms. Without these it becomes very difficult to envisage the emergence of the embryonic alliance between middle classes and working classes, as it is hard to imagine the army disengaging from a regime they had a major part in to side at least temporarily with the protesting masses. And whereas global crises of various sorts as well as examples coming from other Arab countries certainly played a role, they found an extremely fertile socio-economic ground to prosper, leading to the overthrow of an autocrat who had been in power for nearly 30 years.

Whereas the demise of Mubarak was hailed by many as the fall of the main obstacle to democratisation, subsequent developments have had a somewhat sobering effect on these optimistic expectations. The Supreme Council of the Armed Forces, who took power in the wake of Mubarak's oust showed significant reluctance in handing over power to civilians, while at the same time in the last weeks of 2011 launched a full-scale intimidation against NGOs investigating human rights abuses. Rather interestingly in the light of the most recent developments, during the whole transitional period the army unsurprisingly displayed a much stronger concern for preserving their own privileged position than for a genuine democratisation for the country. However, the mobilisation of middle and lower classes was there to stay, and continued despite repressive methods being used extensively, most notably at Maspero in October 2011 when at least 25 demonstrators calling for SCAF's dissolution were killed in clashes with the military police.

Events in early 2012 signalled the distance the army was willing to go in order to meet the demands of protesters. Not very far, to be entirely honest. On the one hand, the state of emergency was finally lifted in January 2012, once legislative power was transferred to the newly elected parliament, where the Freedom and Justice Party (FJP) created by the Muslim Brotherhood had a relative majority of seats. On the other hand,

DOI: 10.1057/9781137395924

the suspension of the assembly tasked with writing a new constitution in April 2012, just one month before the first round of presidential elections, meant that the new president would be elected without a constitution being in place. While arguably aimed at preventing a constitution written by an Islamist-dominated assembly, this measure pushed the Muslim Brotherhood to field its own presidential candidate, something that until that moment they appeared to have no intention of doing.

While somehow surprising for most of the mainstream media, Morsi's election followed in the tracks of FJP's parliamentary victory, further demonstrating the remarkable organisational power of the Muslim Brotherhood when it came to getting their supporters to cast a ballot. At the same time, it is extremely interesting that the first two free elections were won by the group more reluctant to join the 25 January protests, jumping on the bandwagon only when Mubarak's grip on power appeared ever more precarious.

Other than attesting to the organisational skills of the Brotherhood, this outcome can also be traced back to the lack of a strong leadership able to articulate revolutionary demands beyond the demise of Mubarak. The inability of protesting middle and lower classes, Muslims and Copts, men and women to create a common organisational platform allowed the 2011 revolution to be 'stolen', as some commentators put it (Rizk 2013), by the opposition group that was better organised, regardless of its purely instrumental entry within the fold of revolutionary forces.

The shambolic mismanagement of power that Morsi displayed during his year in power reminded the Muslim Brotherhood of the vast difference between getting people to vote for you and getting them to support you once you are in power. This is particularly true if one keeps in mind that in the run-off a significant amount of Egyptians voted for Morsi almost exclusively because the alternative candidate, Ahmed Shafiq, was effectively one of Mubarak's lieutenants. Everything that Morsi did during his brief presidential tenure instead showed despise for his voters who did not belong to the Muslim Brotherhood. The one-sidedness of Morsi's policies was so apparent to lead to a rift also with the other main Islamist party in parliament, the Salafist Al Nour (Alim 2013).

Indeed, the whole idea that the Muslim Brotherhood had developed an effective counter-hegemony rooted in Egyptian society, and that this equipped them with the tools to at least partially accommodate popular demands and by this consolidate their grip on power was clearly falsified by the two policy tenets of their brief spell in power. On the one hand,

DOI: 10.1057/9781137395924

there was an attempt to come to terms with the formal and informal institutions characterised as 'the deep state', best embodied in what appeared as a 'non-interference' pact with the army and the security forces (Teti and Gervasio 2013). On the other hand, all the top policy-making positions were occupied by members of the Brotherhood, suggesting that the actual aim was to achieve integration within the regime, rather than pursue its thorough transformation. Indeed, if you are aware of the deep resistances to change within state institutions, you would be more likely to achieve transformative goals by creating broad-based alliances rather than by going at it alone. Either out of interest or of gross miscalculation, the Muslim Brotherhood followed the latter path, with disastrous consequences.

Possibly with the mitigating circumstance that the Muslim Brotherhood encountered much stronger resistance than the capitalist oligarchy from within the old regime, the self-serving attitude of both groups is remarkably similar. This very similarity points once more in the direction of a rising social group that was unable to develop a project that would go beyond the economic–corporate moment. This happened despite the fact that the Muslim Brotherhood could certainly rely on a broader social platform than the capitalist oligarchy led by Gamal Mubarak. Indeed, despite their roots in the wealthy community of 'pious' businessmen, best exemplified by the recently jailed Khairat El Shater, the Muslim Brotherhood did represent also small and medium entrepreneurs, and arguably also sections of the disenfranchised working classes.

The inability to provide at least some measure of satisfaction of popular demands, together with the generalised economic failure, provided the grounds for a new alliance. Even more than in the first revolution, this was founded on a contingent convergence of interests between disparate social groups than in an actual common platform. The groups involved included the activists engaged in the *Tamarrod* (Rebel) campaign, the revolutionary forces already on the frontline during the 2011 revolution, as well as the army and the *feloul* (Mubarak's supporters). The outcome of the 30 June demonstrations, with the army lightning fast in seizing the chance to give an ultimatum to Morsi and eventually depose him only three days after the beginning of protests, is yet another signal of the problems of achieving revolutionary goals when revolutionaries are unable to organise themselves beyond a generic though incredibly successful petition campaign. In fact, the success of the campaign and

DOI: 10.1057/9781137395924

the demonstrations, which outnumbered the ones that in 2011 led to Mubarak's overthrow, played quite clearly in the hands of the army, who took control of the situation installing a new *interim* president and launching a full-scale domestic 'war on terror' against political Islamists.

It is difficult to predict what is going to happen in a situation that is still incredibly fluid, despite the army's attempt to crystallise its newfound grip on power. At the same time, the method of articulation can help us formulate some informed guesses on what are the different options facing Egypt, its rulers and those concerned with the demands of the 2011 revolution. From the perspective of a political economist, what is most striking in the current situation in Egypt is the stark contrast between an ever-changing political scenario and the staggering continuity with respect to the economic policies pursued. This applied both to the Qandil cabinet appointed by Morsi after his election, and to the current transitional government headed by the liberal economist Hazem El Beblawy. The only arguable transformation with respect to the functioning of the national economy is to be found in the shifting networks of support and patronage in the region, with Qatar strongly supporting Morsi, and currently Saudi Arabia and Kuwait doing the same with the transitional regime and its strategy of stabilisation by scaremongering and repression.

The continuity with respect to economic policies should not lead us to rule out the chances of a rollback towards an *étatist* accumulation regime. However, it is not unlikely that the current situation with respect to the openness of the Egyptian economy will be preserved, only to serve the interests of the military faction within the ruling bloc. More specifically, this will mean that the practice of joint-ventures with transnational capital would still take place, but with the position of Egyptian private capitalists being now taken by the army itself or by the section of large capitalists who did not follow Gamal's challenge to the army (Marshall and Stacher 2012). Thus, regardless of the nationalist rhetoric deployed towards the stalled agreement with the IMF, there is a significant chance of seeing the development of some form of 'neoliberalism without neoliberals'.[1]

Revolutionaries will not find much comfort in current developments with respect to the likely form of the political regime. Three of these developments appear particularly worrying for the prospects of democracy. Firstly, the shutdown of TV channels considered supportive of Morsi and the intimidations against Al Jazeera Egypt suggests that after

DOI: 10.1057/9781137395924

all the army might not be interested in an open debate, and certainly not in one where Islamists are treated as peers and allowed to freely express their views. These forms of coercion have been accompanied by a thorough realignment of other TV stations to the dominant discourse propagated by the army. This discourse is founded on the one hand on considering army's intervention to oust Morsi as the necessary coercive moment to make the revolutionary will come true, and on the other hand on criminalising Morsi and his supporters to the point of redefining them as 'terrorist'. Importantly, this uncritical acceptance of the dominant discourse has taken place both in public and private TV stations, with OnTV owned by the already mentioned tycoon Naguib Sawiris playing a major role in this process.

Secondly, and following from the criminalisation of Islamists, the army and the police have started an aggressive campaign of repression against the sit-ins organised by the Muslim Brotherhood. This has led to an ever-increasing frequency and intensity of violent clashes, which has culminated in the killing of more than one hundred Morsi supporters in Cairo on 27 July, followed a few days later by the government's call on the police to disperse protesters by all means necessary. Similarly, the decision to jail the Brotherhood's leaders on vague charges, freeze their assets and most recently outlaw them and their activities suggests that the process of stabilisation is being managed with payback in mind much more than the actual 'national reconciliation' often mentioned by the *interim* president Mansour.

Thirdly, the new constitutional declaration, hastily presented to the public only five days after Morsi's oust, appears to put together the worse of the pre-revolutionary and the 2012 constitutions. The new 33-article declaration leads to a significant retrenchment in terms of civil and political liberties, effectively providing cover for exceptional emergency measures from nationalisations to prosecution of opposition figures (NCHRL 2013), and moving decision-making power back from the parliament in the hands of the president. At the same time, in order not to alienate entirely the support of Al Nour, which supported the army in the move to depose Morsi, most of the Islamic law articles contained in the 2012 constitution have been preserved (Al-Arian 2013).

If this is the current political situation, does this signal a return to the *status quo ante*? On the one hand, it would seem that the revolution has been stolen for good, and this time by the very actor with the coercive power that had allowed revolutionaries to achieve some results in the

DOI: 10.1057/9781137395924

past. Pressures on the army by international actors concerned with Egypt actually becoming a democracy might prove crucial in this respect, but given the recent record on democracy promotion, one might be forgiven for not putting too much hope on such pressures actually materialising. On the other hand, despite the army's attempts at restabilising the situation at all costs and despite its recently refound popular support, instability is likely to persist for a while. Furthermore, the systematic resort to coercion should be read as a sign of weakness, as the symbol of a fierce rather than a strong regime, to paraphrase Ayubi (1995). After all, as Gramsci taught us, coercion is used more and more often when rulers are unable to win the consent of the ruled, or at least to elicit their acquiescence.

Despite the central position reasserted by the army, the outcome of the current situation is still entirely open-ended. On the one hand, even if a transfer of power to civilians might take place in the short to medium term, the new president would most likely be still subject to the whims of the army. This would not necessarily prevent the new political regime from succeeding in the establishment of an accumulation regime able to generate more revenues than the current one. It does not take much, after all. This might happen either because of productivity gains or because of increased rents. Part of these revenues might then be distributed beyond the ruling bloc into wider society. Such a strategy might somehow appease the masses and gain acquiescence to the existing order of things. This scenario cannot be ruled out, particularly as the army has already demonstrated to be eminently able to read the people's mood and turn it to its own advantage. While this would already be an improvement compared to the Morsi presidency, it would be unlikely to be sustained in the long run, particularly as it is currently extremely difficult to envisage the ideational component necessary to stabilise the uneven distribution of power within Egyptian society, and make it acceptable to subaltern groups.

If this scenario was not to materialise, protests would most likely continue, and for the regime it would become increasingly hard to label as terrorists protesters who have no allegiance whatsoever with Islamist movements. Furthermore, Egypt is not North Korea. Its strategic importance and the coverage that events there are currently receiving would make a regime entirely based on repression and terror untenable in the long run. At the same time, sustained repression would further expose the lack of consent underpinning the new regime. One would hope that during this phase the struggle for unity within the democratic revolutionary spectrum will succeed in developing an agenda able to draw the consent of its many components beyond the mere overthrow of the ruler of the day. This might finally put Egyptian revolutionaries in the position to fulfil the demands of bread, dignity and social justice that brought them to Tahrir Square nearly three years ago.

Note

1   During the wave of political liberalisation that swept the Arab world, during the mid-1990s, Salamé edited a book titled *Democracy without Democrats* (1994). Eventually this liberalisation from above subsided, followed by a new wave of de-liberalisation (Kienle 2001). This is arguably because electoral procedures do not make a democracy, particularly if those changing such procedures have only to lose from a full-fledged democratisation. In this respect, it is instead possible to get to 'neoliberalism without neoliberals', given that transnational capital can always replace local capital, as long as secure property rights, sound money and functioning markets are in place (Harvey 2005: 3).

DOI: 10.1057/9781137395924

References

Abdel-Khalek, Gouda (2001), *Stabilization and Adjustment in Egypt: Reform or De-Industrialization?*, Cheltenham: Edward Elgar.

Alim, Frida (2013), 'The Politics of the Brotherhood Democracy: How the Muslim Brotherhood Burned Their Bridges', 19 July (first access on 24 July), available online at: http://www.jadaliyya.com/pages/index/13062/the-politics-of-the-brotherhood-democracy_how-the-.

Amin, Galal A. (2000), *Whatever Happened to the Egyptians? Changes in Egyptian Society from 1950 to Present*, Cairo: American University in Cairo Press.

——— (2011), *Egypt in the Era of Hosni Mubarak, 1981–2011*, Cairo: American University in Cairo Press.

Arab Republic of Egypt (ARE) (1991), 'Law No. 203 of 1991 Promulgating the Public Business Sector Companies Law and Its Executive Regulations', *Official Gazette*, 28/1991, Cairo, 26 July.

——— (1992a), 'Law No. 95 of 1992 Promulgating the Law of Capital Market', *Official Gazette*, 25/1992, Cairo, 22 June.

——— (1992b), 'Law No. 96 of 1992 Promulgating the Law for Regulating the Relationship between Owner and Tenant', *Official Gazette*, 25/1992, Cairo, 22 June.

Al-Arian, Abdullah (2013), 'Egypt: Dr Frankenstein's Constitution', 10 July (first access on 17 July), available online at: http://www.aljazeera.com/indepth/opinion/2013/07/201371011199459549.html.

DOI: 10.1057/9781137395924

Al Aswany, Alaa (2007), *The Yacoubian Building*, translated by Humphrey Davis, London: Harper Perennial.

—— (2011), *On the State of Egypt: What Caused the Revolution*, Edinburgh: Canongate.

Ayubi, Nazih H. (1995), *Over-stating the Arab State: Politics and Society in the Middle East*, London: I.B. Tauris.

Babb, Sarah (2001), *Managing Mexico: Economists from Nationalism to Neoliberalism*, Princeton, NJ: Princeton University Press.

—— (2005), 'The Rise of the New Money Doctors in Mexico', in Gerald A. Epstein, ed., *Financialization and the World Economy*, Cheltenham: Edward Elgar, 243–259.

Beinin, Joel (2007), 'The Egyptian Workers Movement in 2007', in Hadjar Aouardji et Hélène Legeay, eds, *Chroniques égyptiennes 2007*, Cairo: Centre d'Études et de Documentation Économiques, Juridiques et Sociales.

Beinin, Joel and Hossam El-Hamalawy (2007a), 'Egyptian Textile Workers Confront the New Economic Order', *Middle East Report Online*, 25 March 2007 (first access on 6 October 2010), available online at: http://www.merip.org/mero/mero032507.

—— (2007b), 'Strikes in Egypt Spread from Center of Gravity', *Middle East Report Online*, 9 May 2007 (first access on 6 October 2010), available online at: http://www.merip.org/mero/mero050907.

Binder, Leonard (1978), *In a Moment of Enthusiasm: Political Power and the Second Stratum in Egypt*, Chicago: University of Chicago Press.

Bobbio, Norberto (1958), 'Note sulla dialettica in Gramsci', in Istituto Gramsci, ed., *Studi Gramsciani*, Rome: Editori Riuniti, 73–86.

Bradley, John R. (2008), *Inside Egypt: The Land of the Pharaohs on the Brink of a Revolution*, New York: Palgrave Macmillan.

Bruff, Ian (2008), *Culture and Consensus in European Varieties of Capitalism: A 'Common Sense' Analysis*, Basingstoke: Palgrave Macmillan.

Brynen, Rex (2000), *A Very Political Economy: Peacebuilding and Foreign in the West Bank and Gaza*, Washington, DC: United States Institute of Peace.

Burnham, Peter (1991), 'Neo-Gramscian Hegemony and the International Order', *Capital & Class*, 45: 73–93.

—— (1994), 'Open Marxism and Vulgar International Political Economy', *Review of International Political Economy*, 1(2): 221–231.

DOI: 10.1057/9781137395924

Bush, Ray (1999), *Economic Crisis and the Politics of Reform in Egypt*, Boulder, CO: Westview Press.

—— (2000), 'An Agricultural Strategy without Farmers: Egypt's Countryside in the New Millennium', *Review of African Political Economy*, 27(84): 235–249.

—— (2003), 'Poverty and Neo-Liberal Bias in the Middle East and North Africa', *Development and Change*, 35(4): 673–695.

—— (2007), 'Politics, Power and Poverty: Twenty Years of Agricultural Reform and Market Liberalisation in Egypt', *Third World Quarterly*, 28(7): 1599–1615.

Cammack, Paul A. (1997), *Capitalism and Democracy in the Third World: The Doctrine for Political Development*, Leicester: Leicester University Press.

Cardoso, Fernando Henrique (1979), *Dependency and Development in Latin America*, Berkeley, CA: University of California Press.

—— (1986). 'Entrepreneurs and the Transition Process: The Brazilian Case', in Guillermo O'Donnell, Philippe Schmitter and Laurence Whitehead, eds., *Transition from Authoritarian Rule, Volume 3: Comparative Perspectives*, Baltimore, MD: Johns Hopkins University Press, pp. 137–153.

Chang, Ha-Joon (2002), *Kicking Away the Ladder: Development Strategy in Historical Perspective*, London: Anthem Press.

Chwieroth, Jeffrey M. (2010), *Capital Ideas: The IMF and the Rise of Financial Liberalization*, Princeton, NJ: Princeton University Press.

Collombier, Virginie (2006), 'Le Parti National Démocratique (PND) et le système politique égyptien contemporain: quel rôle pour le parti hégémonique dans le stratégies de consolidation due régime autoritaire', CERI-Sciences Po, November.

Cook, Steven A. (2012), *The Struggle for Egypt: From Nasser to Tahrir Square*, Washington, DC: Council for Foreign Relations.

Cox Michael, ed. (1999), *Rethinking the Soviet Collapse: The Death of Communism and the New Russia*, London: Pinter.

Cox, Robert W. (1981), 'Social Forces, States and World Orders: Beyond International Relations Theory', *Millennium: Journal of International Studies*, 10(2): 126–155.

—— (1983), 'Gramsci, Hegemony and International Relations: An Essay in Method', *Millennium: Journal of International Studies*, 12(2): 162–175.

DOI: 10.1057/9781137395924

———(1987), *Production, Power and World Order: Social Forces in the Making of History*, New York: Columbia University Press.

———(1992), 'Global Perestroika', in Ralph Miliband and Leo Panitch, eds, *The Socialist Register: New World Order?*, London: Merlin Press, 26–43.

Dodge, Toby (2006), 'The Sardinian, the Texan and the Tikriti: Gramsci, the Comparative Autonomy of the State in the Middle East and Regime Change in Iraq', *International Politics*, 43(4): 453–473.

Economist Intelligence Unit (EIU) (1994), *Country Report: Egypt*, London: Economist Intelligence Unit.

———(1996), *Country Report: Egypt*, February, London: Economist Intelligence Unit.

———(2003), *Country Report: Egypt*, February, London: Economist Intelligence Unit.

———(2005), *Country Report: Egypt*, November, London: Economist Intelligence Unit.

———(2006), *Country Profile: Egypt*, London: Economist Intelligence Unit.

———(2010), *Country Report: Egypt, December 2010*, London: Economist Intelligence Unit.

Elasrag, Hussein (2010), 'The Impact of the Informal Sector on the Egyptian Economy', unpublished paper, Cairo: Ministry of Industry and Trade.

El Mahdi, Alia and Ali Rashed (2009), 'The Changing Environment and the Development of Micro- and Small Enterprises in Egypt', in Ragui Assaad, ed., *The Egyptian Labor Market Revisited*, Cairo: American University in Cairo Press, 87–116.

El-Mahdi, Rabab and Philip Marfleet, eds (2009), *Egypt: The Moment of Change*, London: Zed Books.

El-Ghobashi, Mona (2011), 'The Praxis of the Egyptian Revolution', *Middle East Report*, 258 (Spring).

Ezzel Arab, Abdel Aziz (2002), *European Control and Egypt's Traditional Elites: A Case Study in Elite Economic Nationalism*, Lewinston, NY: Edwin Mellen Press.

Farah, Nadia R. (2009), *Egypt's Political Economy: Power Relations in Development*, Cairo: American University in Cairo Press.

Femia, Joseph (1981), *Gramsci's Political Thought: Hegemony, Consciousness and the Revolutionary Process*, Oxford: Clarendon Press.

DOI: 10.1057/9781137395924

Fergany, Nader (2002), 'Poverty and Unemployment in Rural Egypt', in Ray Bush, ed., *Counter-Revolution in Egypt's Countryside: Land and Farmers in the Era of Economic Reform*, London: Zed Books, 211–232.

George, Alexander and Andrew Bennett (2005), *Case Studies and Theory Development in the Social Sciences*, Cambridge, MA: MIT Press.

Gerges, Fawaz (2011), 'Morning After: Egyptians Must Not Lower Their Guard', *The Hill*, 15 February 2011 (first access on 17 February 2011), available online at: http://thehill.com/blogs/congress-blog/foreign-policy/144155-morning-after-egyptians-must-not-lower-their-guard.

Germain, Randall and Michael Kenny (1998), 'Engaging Gramsci: International Relations Theory and the New Gramscians', *Review of International Studies*, 24(1): 3–21.

Gill, Stephen (1990), *American Hegemony and the Trilateral Commission*, Cambridge: Cambridge University Press.

—— (1995), 'Globalisation, Market Civilisation and Disciplinary Neoliberalism', *Millennium: Journal of International Studies*, 24(3): 399–423.

Ghonim, Wael (2012), *Revolution 2.0: The Power of the People Is Greater than the People in Power*, New York: Fourth Estate.

Golding, Sue (1992), *Gramsci's Democratic Theory: Contributions to a Post-Liberal Democracy*, Toronto: University of Toronto Press.

Gramsci, Antonio (1971), *Selection from the Prison Notebooks*, edited and translated by Quentin Hoare and Geoffrey Nowell-Smith, London: Lawrence & Wishart.

—— (1975), *Quaderni del carcere*, 4 vols, Turin: Einaudi.

Gray, Kevin (2010), 'Labour and the State in China's Passive Revolution', *Capital & Class*, 34(3): 449–467.

Griffith-Jones, Stephany (2007), 'Implications of Basel II for Stability and Growth in Developing Countries: Proposals for Further Research and Action', Paper prepared for IBASE Rio Meeting on Financial Liberalisation and Global Governance: The Role of International Entities, 19–20 March, Rio de Janeiro.

Haggard, Stephan and Robert Kaufman, eds (1992), *The Politics of Economic Adjustment: International Constraints, Distributive Conflicts and the State*, Princeton, NJ: Princeton University Press.

Hall, Peter (1993), 'Policy Paradigms, Social Learning, and the State: The Case of Economic Policy Making in Britain', *Comparative Politics*, 25(3): 275–296.

DOI: 10.1057/9781137395924

Hall, Stuart (1996), 'On Postmodernism and Articulation', in David Morley and Kuan-Hsing Chen, eds, *Stuart Hall: Critical Dialogues in Cultural Studies*, London: Routledge, 131–150.

—— (1997), 'Culture and Power: Stuart Hall interviewed by Peter Osborne', *Radical Philosophy* 86: 24–41.

Halliday, Fred (2002), 'The Middle East and the Politics of Differential Integration', in Toby Dodge and Richard Higgott, eds, *Globalisation and the Middle East: Islam, Economy, Society and Politics*, London: Royal Institute of International Affairs, 42–45.

Harris, David (1993), *From Class Struggle to the Politics of Pleasure: The Effects of Gramscianism on Cultural Studies*, London: Routledge.

Harvey, David (1989), *The Condition of Postmodernity*, Oxford: Blackwell.

—— (2005), *A Brief History of Neoliberalism*, Oxford: Oxford University Press.

Heydemann, Steven (1992), 'The Political Logic of Economic Rationality: Selective Stabilization in Syria', in Henry Barkey, ed., *The Politics of Economic Reform in the Middle East*, New York: St. Martin's Press, 11–39.

—— (2004), 'Networks of Privilege: Rethinking the Politics of Economic Reform in the Middle East', in Heydemann, Steven, ed., *Networks of Privilege: The Politics of Economic Reforms Revisited*, Basingstoke: Palgrave Macmillan, 1–34.

Hinnebusch, Raymond A. (1985), *Egyptian Politics under Sadat: The Post-Populist Development of an Authoritarian-Modernizing State*, Cambridge: Cambridge University Press.

—— (1993), 'Class, State and the Reversal of Egypt's Agrarian Reform', *Middle East Report*, 184: 20–23.

—— (2006), 'Authoritarian Persistence, Democratization Theory and the Middle East: An Overview and Critique', *Democratization*, 13(3): 373–395.

Hoare, Quentin and Geoffrey Nowell Smith (1971), 'Problems of Marxism: Introduction', in Antonio Gramsci, *Selections from the Prison Notebooks*, ed. Quentin Hoare and Geoffrey Nowell Smith, London: Lawrence & Wishart, 378–380.

Hobsbawm, Eric (1987), *The Age of Empire, 1875–1914*, London: Weidenfeld & Nicholson.

Huntington, Samuel P. (1991), *The Third Wave: Democratization in the Late Twentieth Century*, Norman, OK: University of Oklahoma Press.

DOI: 10.1057/9781137395924

Ikram, Khalid (2006), *The Egyptian Economy, 1952–2000: Performance, Policies, Issues*, London: Routledge.

International Monetary Fund (IMF) (1993a), *Arab Republic of Egypt – Second Review of Stand-by Arrangement*, EBS/93/7, 13 January.

——(1993b), 'Egypt: Extended Fund Facility', *IMF Survey*, 11 October, 313.

——(1997), 'The Egyptian Stabilization Experience: An Analytical Retrospective', prepared by Arvind Subramanian, *IMF Working Papers*, WP/97/105, Washington, DC: International Monetary Fund.

——(1998), 'Egypt: Beyond Stabilization, Towards a Dynamic Market Economy', *IMF Occasional Paper*, 163, Washington, DC: International Monetary Fund.

——(1999), *External Evaluation of Surveillance: Report by a Group of Independent Experts*, Washington, DC: International Monetary Fund.

——(2003), 'IMF Welcomes Arab Republic of Egypt's Decision to Adopt a Floating Exchange Rate Regime', *Press Release No. 03/12*, 30 January, Washington: International Monetary Fund.

Jadaliyya (2013), 'Military-Business Alliances in Egypt Before and after 30 June: Interview with Wael Gamal', 20 July (first access on 21 July), available online at: http://www.jadaliyya.com/pages/index/13070/military-business-alliances-in-egypt-before-and-af.

Jessop, Bob (1982), *The Capitalist State: Marxist Theories and Methods*, Oxford: Blackwell.

——(1990), *State Theory: Putting the Capitalist State in Its Place*, Cambridge: Polity Press.

——(2010), 'World Market, World State, World Society: Marxian Insights and Scientific Realist Investigations', in Jonathan Joseph and Colin Wight, eds, *Scientific Realism and International Relations*, Basingstoke: Palgrave Macmillan, 186–202.

Joseph, Jonathan (2010), 'The International as Emergent: Challenging Old and New Orthodoxies in International Relations Theory', in Jonathan Joseph and Colin Wight, eds, *Scientific Realism and International Relations*, Basingstoke: Palgrave Macmillan, 51–68.

Khalil, Ashraf (2011), *Liberation Square: Inside the Egyptian Revolution and the Rebirth of a Nation*, London: St Martin's Press.

Khalil, Karima (2011), *Messages from Tahrir: Signs from the Egyptian Revolution*, Cairo: American University in Cairo Press.

Kienle, Eberhard (2001), *A Grand Delusion: Democracy and Economic Reform in Egypt*, London: I.B. Tauris.

DOI: 10.1057/9781137395924

—— (2003), 'Domesticating Economic Liberalization: Controlled Market-Building in Contemporary Egypt', in Eberhard Kienle, ed., *Politics from Above, Politics from Below: The Middle East in the Age of Economic Reform*, London: Saqi, 144–156.

Laclau, Ernesto and Chantal Mouffe (2001), *Hegemony and Socialist Strategy: Towards a Radical Democratic Politics*, 2nd edn, London: Verso.

Lagi, Marco, Karla Z. Bertrand and Yaneer Bar-Yam (2011), 'The Food Crisis and Political Instability in North Africa and the Middle East', New England Complex Systems Institute (first access on 23 January 2012), available online at: http://necsi.edu/research/social/ food_crises.pdf.

Levi, Margaret (1988), *Of Rule and Revenue*, Berkeley, CA: University of California Press.

Levy, Jack (2008), 'Case Studies: Types, Designs, and Logics of Inference', *Conflict Management and Peace Science*, 25(1): 1–18.

Linz, Juan J. (1964), 'An Authoritarian Regime: Spain', in Erik Allardt and Yrjö Littanen, eds., *Cleavages, Ideology and Party Systems: Contributions to Political Sociology*, New York: Academic Bookstore.

Lipschutz, Ronnie D. (1992), 'Reconstructing World Politics: The Emergence of Global Civil Society', *Millennium: Journal of International Studies*, 21(3): 389–420.

Lipset, Seymour M. (1959), 'Some Social Requisites of Democracy: Economic Development and Political Legitimacy', *American Political Science Review*, 53(1): 69–105.

Luciani, Giacomo (2007), 'Linking Economic and Political Reform in the Middle East: The Role of the Bourgeoisie', in Oliver Schlumberger, ed., *Debating Arab Authoritarianism: Dynamics and Durability in Nondemocratic Regimes*, Stanford, CA: Stanford University Press, 161–176.

Luporini, Cesare (1958), 'La metodologia filosofica del marxismo nel pensiero di A. Gramsci: Appunti', in Istituto Gramsci, ed., *Studi Gramsciani*, Rome: Editori Riuniti, 37–46.

Marshall, Shana, and Joshua Stacher (2012), 'Egypt's Generals and Transnational Capital', *Middle East Report*, 42(262), Spring, first accessed: 22 June 2012, available online at: http://www.merip.org/ mer/mer262/egypts-generals-transnational-capital.

DOI: 10.1057/9781137395924

Martins, Luciano (1986), 'The "Liberalization" of Authoritarian Rule in Brazil', in Guillermo O'Donnell, Philippe Schmitter and Laurence Whitehead, eds., *Transition from Authoritarian Rule, Volume 2: Latin America*, Baltimore, MD: Johns Hopkins University Press, pp. 72–94.

Masoud, Tarek (2010), 'Is Gamal Mubarak the Best Hope for Egyptian Democracy?', *Foreign Policy*, 20 September 2010 (first access on 22 September 2010), available online at: http://mideast.foreignpolicy.com/posts/2010/09/20/is_gamal_mubarak_the_best_hope_for_egyptian_democracy_0.

Middle East Economic Digest (MEED) (1997), 'Land Reform Heralds New Era in Egyptian Agriculture', *Middle East Economic Digest*, 3 October.

Ministry of Agriculture and Land Reclamation (MALR), *Agriculture Census 2000*, Cairo: Ministry of Agriculture and Land Reclamation.

Mitchell, Timothy (1999), 'Dreamland: The Neoliberalism of Your Desires', *Middle East Report*, 210 (Spring): 28–33.

——— (2002), *Rule of Experts: Egypt, Techno-politics, Modernity*, Berkeley, CA: University of California Press.

Mohieldin, Mahmoud and Sahar Nasr (2003), 'On Bank Privatization in Egypt', *ERF Working Papers Series*, 03/25, Cairo: Economic Research Forum.

——— (2007), 'On Bank Privatization: The Case of Egypt', *Quarterly Review of Economics and Finance*, 46(5): 707–725.

Moktar, May and Jackline Wahba (2002), 'Informalization of Labor in Egypt', in Ragui Assaad, ed., *The Egyptian Labor Market in an Era of Reform*, Cairo: American University in Cairo Press, 131–157.

Momani, Bessma (2005), 'IMF-Egyptian Debt Negotiations', *Cairo Papers in Social Science*, 26(3), Cairo: American University in Cairo Press.

Moore, Phoebe (2007), *Globalisation and Labour Struggle in Asia: A Neo-Gramscian Critique of South Korean Political Economy*, London: I.B. Tauris.

Morton, Adam David (2005), 'A Double Reading of Gramsci: Beyond the Logic of Contingency', *Critical Review of International Social and Political Philosophy*, 8(4): 439–453.

——— (2007), *Unravelling Gramsci: Hegemony and Passive Revolution in the Global Political Economy*, London: Pluto Press.

——— (2011), *Revolution and State in Modern Mexico: The Political Economy of Uneven Development*, Boulder, CO: Rowman & Littlefield.

DOI: 10.1057/9781137395924

Munck, Geraldo L. (1996), 'Disaggregating Political Regime: Conceptual Issues in the Study of Democratization', *Kellogg Institute for International Affairs Working Papers*, WP228, Notre Dame, IN: University of Notre Dame.

Murphy, Craig (1994), *International Organizations and Industrial Change*, Cambridge: Cambridge University Press.

National Community for Human Rights and Law (NCHRL) (2013), 'An Authoritarian and Deceptive Constitutional Declaration', 11 July.

Nelson, Joan M., ed. (1989), *Fragile Coalitions: The Politics of Economic Adjustment*, Washington, DC: Overseas Development Institute.

Noland, Marcus and Howard Pack (2005), 'The East Asian Industrial Policy Experience: Implications for the Middle East', *ECES Working Papers Series*, WP106, Cairo: Egyptian Center for Economic Studies.

Nuns, Alex, and Nadia Idle, eds (2011), *Tweets from Tahrir: Egypt's Revolution as It Unfolded, in the Words of the People Who Made It*, London: OR Books.

OANDA (2011), 'Historical Exchange Rates' (first access on 16 January 2011), available online at: http://www.oanda.com/currency/historical-rates/.

Odell, John S. (2001), 'Case Study Methods in International Political Economy', *International Studies Perspectives*, 2(1): 161–176.

O'Donnell, Guillermo, Philippe Schmitter and Lawrence Whitehead, eds (1986), *Transitions from Authoritarian Rule*, 4 vols, Baltimore, MD: Johns Hopkins University Press.

Osman, Tarek (2010), *Egypt on the Brink: From Nasser to Mubarak*, New Haven, CT: Tale University Press.

—— (2011), *Egypt on the Brink: From the Rise of Nasser to the Fall of Mubarak*, New Haven, CT: Yale University Press.

Owen, Roger (2001), 'The Middle Eastern State: Repositioning not Retreat?', in Hassan Hakimian and Ziba Moshaver, eds, *The State and Global Change: The Political Economy of Transition in the Middle East and North Africa*, Richmond: Curzon, 232–247.

Perthes, Volker (2004), 'Politics and Elite Change in the Arab World', in Volker Perthes, ed., *Arab Elites: Negotiating the Politics of Change*, Boulder, CO: Lynne Rienner, 1–32.

Piccone, Paul (1976), 'From Spaventa to Gramsci', *Telos*, 31: 35–65.

Pratt, Nicola (2005), 'Identity, Culture and Democratization: The Case of Egypt', *New Political Science*, 27(1): 69–86.

DOI: 10.1057/9781137395924

Refaat, Amal (2003), 'Trade-Induced Protectionism in Egypt's Manufacturing Sector', *ECES Working Paper Series*, WP88, Cairo: Egyptian Center for Economic Studies.

Richards, Alan (1991), 'The Political Economy of Dilatory Reform: Egypt in the 1980s', *World Development*, 19(12): 1721–1730.

Rizk, Philip (2013), Is the Egyptian Revolution Dead?', *Jadaliyya*, 11 July (first access on 13 July), available online at: http://www.jadaliyya.com/pages/index/12895/is-the-egyptian-revolution-dead-.

Richter, Frederik (2006), 'Finishing Off Law 1991/203 and Beyond: The Egyptian Privatization Programme During 2005', in Florian Kohstall, ed., *L'Égypte dans l'année 2005*, Cairo: CEDEJ (first access on 26 November 2010), available online at: http://www.cedej-eg.org/spip.php?article133.

Robinson, William I. (2003), *Transnational Conflicts: Central America, Social Change and Globalization*, London: Verso.

——— (2004), *A Theory of Global Capitalism: Production, Class and State in a Transnational World*, Baltimore, MD: Johns Hopkins University Press.

Roccu, Roberto (2013), 'David Harvey in Tahrir Square: The Discontented, the Dispossessed and the Egyptian Revolution', *Third World Quarterly*, 34(3): 423–440.

Rodrik, Dani (2006), 'Goodbye Washington Consensus, Hello Washington Confusion?', *Journal of Economic Literature*, 44(4): 973–987.

Roll, Stephan (2010), ' "Finance Matters!" The Influence of Financial Sector Reforms on the Development of the Entrepreneurial Elite in Egypt', *Mediterranean Politics*, 15(3): 349–370.

Rostow, Walt (1960), *The Stages of Economic Growth: A Non-Communist Manifesto*, Cambridge: Cambridge University Press.

Rupert, Mark (1995), *Producing Hegemony: The Politics of Mass Production and American Global Power*, Cambridge: Cambridge University Press.

Rushdy, Hatem, ed. (2011), *18 Days in Tahrir: Stories from Egypt's Revolution*, London: Havens Books.

Saad, Reem (2002), 'Egyptian Politics and the Tenancy Law', in Ray Bush, ed., *Counter-Revolution in Egypt's Countryside: Land and Farmers in the Era of Economic Reform*, London: Zed Books, 103–126.

Sadowski, Yahya M. (1991), *Political Vegetables? Businessman and Bureaucrat in the Development of Egyptian Agriculture*, Washington, DC: The Brookings Institution.

DOI: 10.1057/9781137395924

Said, Mona (2009), 'The Fall and Rise in Wage Inequality in Egypt: New Evidence from the Egyptian Labor Market Panel Survey 2006', in Ragui Assaad, ed., *The Egyptian Labor Market Revisited*, Cairo: American University in Cairo Press, 53–82.

Salamé, Ghassan, ed. (1994), *Democracy without Democrats? The Renewal of Politics in the Muslim World*, London: I.B. Tauris.

Sassoon, Anne Showstack (2001), 'Globalisation, Hegemony and Passive Revolution', *New Political Economy*, 6(1): 5–17.

Schlumberger, Oliver (2004), 'Patrimonial Capitalism: Economic Reform and Economic Order in the Arab World', PhD dissertation in Political Science, University of Tubingen.

——— (2008), 'Structural Reform, Economic Order, and Development: Patrimonial Capitalism', *Review of International Political Economy*, 15(4): 622–645.

Shams El-Din, Ashraf (1998), 'Capital Market Performance in Egypt: Efficiency, Pricing, and Market-Based Risk Management', in Mohamed El-Erian and Mahmoud Mohieldin, eds, *Financial Development in Emerging Markets: The Egyptian Experience*, Cairo: Egyptian Center for Economic Studies, 147–165.

Shields, Stuart (2012), *The International Political Economy of Transition: Neoliberal Hegemony and Eastern Central Europe's Transformation*, London: Routledge.

Sims, David (2010), *Understanding Cairo: The Logic of a City Out of Control*, Cairo: American University in Cairo Press.

Snyder, Lewis W. (2007), 'The Clash of Mental Models in the Middle East: Neoliberal vs. Islamic Ideas', in Ravi K. Roy, Arthur T. Denzau, and Thomas D. Willett, eds, *Neoliberalism: National and Regional Experiments with Global Ideas*, London: Routledge, 206–228.

Soliman, Samer (2011), *The Autumn of Dictatorship: Fiscal Crisis and Political Change in Egypt under Mubarak*, Princeton, NJ: Princeton University Press.

Soueif, Ahdaf (2012), *Cairo: My City, Our Revolution*, London: Bloomsbury Publishing.

Springborg, Robert (1989), *Mubarak's Egypt: Fragmentation of the Political Order*, Boulder, CO: Westview Press.

Strange, Susan (1988), *State and Markets*, London: Pinter.

Talani, Leila Simona (forthcoming), *The Arab Spring in the Global Political Economy*, Basingstoke: Palgrave Macmillan.

DOI: 10.1057/9781137395924

Teti, Andrea and Gennaro Gervasio (2013), 'The Army's Coup in Egypt: For the People or against the People?', *OpenDemocracy*, 10 July (first access on 16 July), available online at: http://www.opendemocracy. net/andrea-teti-gennaro-gervasio/army%E2%80%99s-coup-in-egypt-for-people-or-against-people.

Tetlock, Philip E. (2006), *Expert Political Judgment: How Good Is It? How Can We Know?*, Princeton, NJ: Princeton University Press.

Tripp, Charles (2001), 'States, Elites and the "Management of Change"', in Hassan Hakimian and Ziba Moshaver, eds, *The State and Global Change: The Political Economy of Transition in the Middle East and North Africa*, Richmond: Curzon, 211–231.

—— (2012), *The Power and the People: Paths of Resistance in the Middle East*, Cambridge: Cambridge University Press.

Van Apeldoorn, Bastian (2002), *Transnational Capitalism and the Struggle Over European Integration*, London: Routledge.

Van der Pijl, Kees (1984), *The Making of an Atlantic Ruling Class*, London: Verso.

—— (1998), *Transnational Classes and International Relations*, London: Routledge.

Vitalis, Robert (1995), *When Capitalists Collide: Business Conflict and the End of Empire in Egypt*, Berkeley, CA: University of California Press.

Wahba, Mourad M. (1994), *The Role of the State in the Egyptian Economy: 1945–1981*, Reading: Ithaca Press.

Wahba, Jackline (2009), 'Informal in Egypt: A Stepping Stone or a Dead End?', *ERF Working Paper Series*, WP 456, Cairo: Economic Research Forum.

Waterbury, John (1983), *The Egypt of Nasser and Sadat: The Political Economy of Two Regimes*, Princeton, NJ: Princeton University Press.

Williamson, John (1989), 'What Washington Means by Policy Reform', in John Williamson, ed., *Latin American Adjustment: How Much Has Happened?*, Washington, DC: Institute for International Economics, 5–24.

World Bank (1993), *Arab Republic of Egypt – An Agricultural Strategy for the 1990s*, Washington, DC: The World Bank.

—— (2001), 'Arab Republic of Egypt - Toward Agricultural Competitiveness in the 21st Century: An Agricultural Export-Oriented Strategy', *Report No. 23405 – EGT*, Washington, DC: The World Bank.

DOI: 10.1057/9781137395924

—— (2006), 'Program Document for a Proposed Loan in the Amount of US$500 million to the Arab Republic of Egypt for a Financial Sector Development Policy Loan', *Report No. 36197 – EG*, Washington, DC: The World Bank.

—— (2007), 'A Poverty Assessment Update', *Report No. 39885 – EG*, Washington, DC: The World Bank.

—— (2008), *Access to Finance and Economic Growth in Egypt*, a study led by Sahar Nasr, Washington, DC: The World Bank.

—— (2010a), *World Development Indicators*, (first accessed on 12 June 2010), available at: http://data.worldbank.org/data-catalog.

—— (2010b), 'Program Document for a Proposed Loan in the Amount of US$500 million to the Arab Republic of Egypt for a Third Financial Sector Development Policy Loan', *Report No. 53277 – EG*, Washington, DC: The World Bank.

—— (2010c), 'World Bank Group President appoints Egyptian Investment Minister as Managing Director', *Press Release No: 2011/081/ EXC*, Washington, DC: The World Bank.

Worth, Owen (2008), 'The Poverty and Potential of Gramscian Thought in International Relations', *International Politics*, 45(6): 633–649.

Wurzel, Ulrich (2009), 'The Political Economy of Authoritarianism in Egypt: Insufficient Structural Reforms, Limited Outcomes and a Lack of New Actors', in Laura Guazzone and Daniela Pioppi, eds, *The Arab State and Neo-Liberal Globalization: The Restructuring of State Power in the Middle East*, Reading: Ithaca Press, 97–123.

Zaalouk, Malak (1989), *Class, Power and Foreign Capital in Egypt: The Rise of the New Bourgeoisie*, London: Zed Books.

Zanardo, Aldo (1958), 'Il "manuale" di Bukharin visto dai comunisti tedeschi e da Gramsci', in Istituto Gramsci, ed., *Studi gramsciani*, Rome: Editori Riuniti, 337–368.

DOI: 10.1057/9781137395924

Index

30 March Programme, 97
30 June demonstrations, 117

Abaza, Amin, 66
accumulation regime, 31–2, 99,
    100, 120
    definition of, 31
    étatist, 31, 39, 73, 97, 118
    neoliberal, 13, 31, 49, 73, 101
    state capitalist, 96
    transformation of, 15, 34, 39,
        72, 95, 98, 111–12
agriculture, 47, 51, 52, 63, 82
Al Jazeera Egypt, 118
Al Nour (Salafist party), 116, 119
American Chamber of
    Commerce in Egypt
    (AmCham), 64, 68, 79, 93
Arab Spring, *see* Arab
    uprisings
Arab uprisings, 3–5, 10, 115
army
    in the revolution, 16, 104,
        115, 117–18, 119
    parallel economy, 37, 65, 70
    predominant position, 8, 69,
        96, 97, 98, 105, 113
articulation
    as determination in the
        first instance and relative
        autonomy, 28, 30, 35, 54
    as method, 19, 24, 26–9, 35,
        40, 72, 73, 108–10, 118
    interscalar, 27, 29, 39, 97,
        100, 110
    of the international and the
        national, 14, 18, 27,
        40–55, 109

of the economic and the
    political, 14, 18, 28, 59–72,
    96, 98, 109
of the material and the
    ideational, 14, 18, 28,
    77–91, 99, 109, 112
Asset Management
    Programme, 44, 53
authoritarianism
    definition of, 31–2
    neoliberal, 69–72, 112
Azmi, Zakaria, 67
Ayubi, Nazih, 18, 69, 73, 95

Bahgat
    family, 61
    Ahmed, 61, 79
Bahrain, 3
banking sector, 42, 46, 63–4,
    71, 84, 88–9, 102
Basel II regulations, 88–9
Bobbio, Norberto, 25
Boghdady, Shafiq, 79
Boutros-Ghali, Youssef, 65, 68,
    79, 85
Brynen, Rex, 62
Bukharin, Mikhail, 25–6

Cairo University, 68
capitalist oligarchy,
    predatory, 13, 59, 69, 77, 90,
        99, 101, 105
    rise of, *see* new business
        class, political rise of
Central Bank of Egypt (CBE),
    11, 71, 89
cognitive bias, 12, 112

DOI: 10.1057/9781137395924

DOI: 10.1057/9781137395924

DOI: 10.1057/9781137395924

DOI: 10.1057/9781137395924

Lightning Source UK Ltd.
Milton Keynes UK
UKOW05n0557281113

221999UK00002B/16/P

9 781137 395917